Better Homes and Gardens®
STEP-BY-STEP
Tiling
Projects

Better Homes and Gardens® Books
Des Moines, Iowa

Better Homes and Gardens® Books
An imprint of Meredith® Books

Step-by-Step Tiling Projects
Editor: Paula Marshall
Associate Art Director: Lynda Haupert
Contributing Copy Editors: Melinda Levine, James Sanders
Contributing Proofreaders: Jeanette Alt, Debra Morris Smith, Margaret Smith
Copy Chief: Catherine Hamrick
Copy and Production Editor: Terri Fredrickson
Electronic Production Coordinator: Paula Forest
Editorial and Design Assistants: Kaye Chabot, Treesa Landry, Karen Schirm
Production Director: Douglas M. Johnston
Production Manager: Pam Kvitne
Assistant Prepress Manager: Marjorie J. Schenkelberg

Produced by Greenleaf Publishing, Inc.
Publishing Director: Dave Toht
Writer: Jeff Beneke
Associate Editor: Steve Cory
Editorial Art Director: Jean DeVaty
Assistant Editor: Rebecca JonMichaels
Design: Melanie Lawson Design
Illustrations: Tony Davis; Brian Gilmer, Art Factory; Greg Maxon

Cover Photograph: Tony Kubat Photography
Production and Back Cover Design: John Seid

Meredith® Books
Editor in Chief: James D. Blume
Design Director: Matt Strelecki
Managing Editor: Gregory H. Kayko
Executive Shelter Editor: Denise L. Caringer

Director, Sales & Marketing, Retail: Michael A. Peterson
Director, Sales & Marketing, Special Markets: Rita McMullen
Director, Sales & Marketing, Home & Garden Center Channel: Ray Wolf
Director, Operations: George A. Susral
Vice President, General Manager: Jamie L. Martin

Better Homes and Gardens® Magazine
Editor in Chief: Jean LemMon
Executive Building Editor: Joan McCloskey

Meredith Publishing Group
President, Publishing Group: Christopher Little
Vice President, Consumer Marketing & Development: Hal Oringer

Meredith Corporation
Chairman and Chief Executive Officer: William T. Kerr
Chairman of the Executive Committee: E. T. Meredith III

All of us at Better Homes and Gardens® Books are dedicated to providing you with information and ideas you need to enhance your home. We welcome your comments and suggestions about this book on tiling. Write to us at: Better Homes and Gardens® Books, Do-It-Yourself Editorial Department, 1716 Locust St., Des Moines, IA 50309–3023.

Note to the Reader: Due to differing conditions, tools, and individual skills, Meredith Corporation assumes no responsibility for any damages, injuries suffered, or losses incurred as a result of following the information published in this book. Before beginning any project, review the instructions carefully, and if any doubts or questions remain, consult local experts or authorities. Because local codes and regulations vary greatly, you always should check with local authorities to ensure that your project complies with all applicable local codes and regulations. Always read and observe all of the safety precautions provided by any tool or equipment manufacturer, and follow all accepted safety procedures.

TABLE OF CONTENTS

INTRODUCTION

Many people think they must hire a professional contractor to install ceramic or stone tile. They assume it takes years of practice and on-the-job experience to correctly install tile. Years ago, tiling installations did require the keen eye and a practiced hand of a professional, but today new materials and techniques are available that make it easier than ever for a do-it-yourselfer to handle most residential installations. While tiling takes patience and some basic do-it-yourself skills, with the right information and proper tools and materials, most homeowners can manage a professional-looking job on their own.

Step-by-Step Tiling Projects provides the information you need to plan and carry out a tiling job. You will learn how to plan the project, how to decide which types of tile to use in different installations, what types of adhesives to choose and how to use them, and how to finish and maintain your project so it will provide you with years of service.

Step-by-Step Tiling Projects will help you decide which jobs you can take on yourself. Even if you decide not to do the job yourself, you will be better equipped to manage the job wisely: Qualified tiling professionals appreciate working with an educated client. If you choose to hire out the job, you will be equipped to find the right contractor, choose the right materials, and get the results you want.

Working to Code

Even though you may be an amateur working on your own house, you have the same responsibilities as a tiling contractor. The tiles and adhesives you use must be rated for your specific installation. The framing and the substrate must be strong enough to support the installation. If the tiles are going to be exposed to moisture, the materials and installation techniques must be waterproof. If the tiles are going outdoors, where they might be subjected to freezing temperatures, the entire job must be planned to cope with such conditions. And when you alter any wiring or plumbing in the course of the project, you must follow the construction requirements of your local building department.

Working with Your Local Building Department

While a modest tiling project, such as resurfacing a kitchen countertop, is unlikely to require a permit, a kitchen or bathroom renovation that involves structural carpentry, plumbing, and wiring in addition to the tile installation likely will require a permit. If you're unsure, play it safe and contact your local building department.

The procedures in this book represent widely accepted techniques and materials, but be aware that local building codes can vary a great deal. Although they may seem bothersome, codes exist to ensure minimal standards of quality and safety are met. Ignoring codes can lead to costly mistakes, health hazards, and even difficulties in selling your house someday. Neglecting to contact your building department could cause you the expense and trouble of tearing out and redoing the work.

There's no telling what kind of advice you will encounter when you apply for a permit or when an inspector visits your site. You may be told that a permit and inspections will not be required, and be done with it. If a permit is needed, an inspector will likely need to look at your work. Some inspectors are helpful, friendly, and flexible; others are real sticklers. But no matter what sort of personality you'll be dealing with, your work will go better if you follow these guidelines:

■ This book is a good place to start, but learn as much as you can about each project before you talk with an inspector from your local building department; you'll avoid miscommuniction and get your permits more quickly. Your building department may have literature concerning your type of installation. If not, consult national codes.
■ Go to your building department with a plan to be approved or amended; don't expect the department's staff to plan the job for you.
■ Present your plan with neatly drawn diagrams and a complete list of the materials you will be using.
■ Be sure you clearly understand when inspections are required. Do not cover up any work that needs to be inspected.
■ Be as courteous as possible. Inspectors are often wary of homeowners because many attempt projects beyond their capabilities. Show the inspector you are serious about doing the job right, and comply with any requirements.

How to Use This Book

Begin by reading the first chapter, "Tile Basics." It provides a detailed overview of the many types of tile available and the pros and cons of using tile in various locations. Using this knowledge, you will be better able to determine whether the project you have in mind makes sense.

Once you know what you want, the next step is to gain an understanding of how to attain it. "Tools and Materials" gives you all the basic information you need on tool selection and how to select the materials you will need in addition to the tiles themselves. The chapter "Tiling Techniques" also should be read from beginning to end before you start your project. There you'll get a brief apprenticeship in tile setting, learn some basic tool skills, and gain an understanding of each of the steps necessary for your project.

"Tiling Projects" presents a series of specific tile installations, complete with the information and guidance you need for each one. This section also will help you to determine the feasibility of tiling plans and assess whether you feel you have the skills to do the job yourself.

Finally, "Repair and Maintenance" offers proven tips on making an old tile installation look new again and ensuring that a new installation doesn't show its age prematurely.

Feature Boxes

In addition to basic instructions, you'll find plenty of tips throughout this book. For every project, a "You'll Need" box tells you how long the project will take, what skills are necessary, and what tools you must have. The other tip boxes shown on this page are scattered throughout the book, providing practical help to ensure that the work you do will be as pleasurable as possible, and that it will result in safe, long-lasting improvements to your home and yard.

TOOLS TO USE

If you'll need special tools not commonly found in a homeowner's toolbox, we'll tell you about them in Tools to Use.

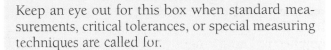

Money $ Saver

Throwing money at a job does not necessarily make it a better one. Money Saver helps cut your costs with tips on how to estimate your material needs accurately, make wise tool purchases, and organize the job to minimize wasted labor.

MEASUREMENTS

Keep an eye out for this box when standard measurements, critical tolerances, or special measuring techniques are called for.

CAUTION!

When a how-to step requires special care, Caution! warns you what to watch out for. It will help keep you from doing damage to yourself or the job at hand.

EXPERTS' INSIGHT

Tricks of the trade can make all the difference in helping you do a job quickly and well. Experts' Insight gives you insiders' tips on how to make the job easier.

USING TILE TODAY

Tile is an ancient material long valued for its durability and nearly limitless decorative potential. Today, new products and installation techniques have made this time-tested material more popular than ever. Tile is now well within the budget and talents of any serious do-it-yourselfer.

The options for color, texture, and shape are so varied that your biggest challenge may be choosing the best products and designs for your project. Begin by scanning books and magazines and visiting tile showrooms to select the colors and patterns that best suit your project. Once you've chosen the colors and patterns, select the type of tile right for the job (see pages 14–17). Compare prices by visiting your local home center or flooring retailer, or by directly contacting tile manufacturers via their Internet sites.

ABOVE: Decorative tile can make a dramatic focal point that lends an impression of durability and quality to a room. A fireplace surround is an ideal place to get full impact from expensive decorative tiles.

ABOVE: This kitchen countertop incorporates a marble pastry slab into a ceramic tile surface. (See page 47 for how to set marble tile.) Grout lines, the area of a tile surface that is the most difficult to clean, are kept to a minimum with 6-inch tiles. Wood edging helps unify the countertop and the kitchen cabinetry.

ABOVE: Ideal for entryways, glazed or sealed tile is moisture resistant, colorfast, and easy to clean. Tile choices are broad enough to suit any style home.

ABOVE: *Ceramic tile is noted for its water-resistant quality—one reason it is used in bathrooms. Tile can be used on floors, walls, and countertops, and it's ideal for shower stalls and around bathtubs. With careful planning, the entire room can be covered in an integrated design.*

If you live in a cool climate, bear in mind that tile flooring can be cold. Consider installing radiant heating in the setting bed (see page 12), an ideal way to keep your tile floor warm underfoot.

ABOVE: *Tile is a protective and decorative material to use around a fireplace or woodstove. See page 91 for precautions to take when installing tiles that will be subject to high temperatures.*

ABOVE: *One of the advantages of tile is that it can be used indoors and outdoors, beautifully merging areas of the home. You'll want to hire a professional to install the tile in a complex pool and patio area like this, but tiling a concrete patio or pool surround is well within the skill range of the average do-it-yourselfer.*

COMBINING STYLE AND DURABILITY

Tile can be imaginatively put to work in all the hardworking areas of your house—almost anywhere you wish to combine utility and beauty. Informal living areas, fireplace surrounds, entryway floors, and of course kitchens and baths are all places where tile can enhance your home. In warm climates, it has long been the material of choice for keeping floors and walls cool and dry. Though expensive initially, the long life and low maintenance of tile usually negate the cost.

Desirable as tile is in many areas of the house, it might not always be the perfect covering for every surface in your home. An overabundance of tile, especially if it is the same color and size, can be overwhelming and clinical-looking.

And in some situations tile's virtues can be a drawback: Tile is unforgiving when breakable objects fall on it. Tile floors can be cold when temperatures drop. Even the acoustic effect of tile should be kept in mind. Tile is great for singing in the shower but can create unpleasant echoes in large living areas.

ABOVE RIGHT: Heavily trafficked informal living areas with access to the outdoors need a utilitarian but attractive surface. Tile makes a hard-working transition between indoors and outdoors and a pleasantly neutral setting for a variety of furnishing styles.

RIGHT: For an eye-catching focal point in a room, use tile to cover and decorate a fireplace, or to grace the surfaces around a woodstove. In otherwise bland rooms, ornamental tile work like this is all the architectural detail a room needs.

RIGHT: Want protection from whatever the kids can track in—without sacrificing style? Even a backdoor entryway is a place where you'll want to put your best foot forward with beautiful, low-maintenance tile. It will withstand lots of abuse but can be cleaned up quickly and thoroughly. Although small in terms of square footage, entryways make a strong style statement—ideal places to invest in a tile installation.

BELOW: In bathrooms, tile protects underlying surfaces from water damage while offering additional safety and convenience. You can create a comfortable and handy place to sit in a shower stall or around a tub. In bathrooms and other wet areas, be sure to choose tiles with a slip-resistant surface. Around tubs and showers, consider using smaller tiles, or even mosaics; the additional grout required by these tiles will make the floor less slippery.

USING DECORATIVE TILE

When designing a tile installation, don't just think in terms of individual tiles. Instead, think of the whole surface and of adjacent surfaces, textures, and colors. You can be decorative without having to rely heavily on decorative tiles.

If you want to use specially decorated tiles, be sure they are integrated with the overall scheme. You often can buy decorative tiles to match the colors and sizes of the manufacturer's regular tiles. If you decide to use a few hand-painted tiles in a wall of commercially produced tiles, make sure the sizes and the colors of the tiles are compatible. If you plan to have a tile artist produce custom work for you, be sure to discuss the colors and function of the total project.

ABOVE: Tile is one of the few materials that can stand up to daily use in heavily traveled household areas while adding beautiful design detail. Decorative tiles can be costly, but fortunately a few can go a long way toward beautifying a room, and choosing them can be great fun.

ABOVE: Used to good effect, this beautiful but quirky pieced-together tile job uses a mix of tiles to make colorful borders. This is a creative way to use the wide range of decorative tiles available, but be aware that if you mix tiles from different manufacturers, sizes and thicknesses can vary. You may find installation will be more complicated.

Money $ Saver

DESIGN WITHIN BUDGET

Because decorative and trim tiles can cost substantially more than regular field tiles, plan ahead to keep the finishing touches from destroying your budget. The secret is avoiding the excessive use of the high-priced tiles. For example, just a few hand-painted or marble tiles mixed in among regular tiles will be more effective than scores of tiles clamoring for attention. While patterned border tiles can look great around the perimeters, you can achieve a similar effect using regular tiles in a different color. Limit the use of your more expensive tiles and they will be more likely to stand out and attract attention.

USING TILE OUTDOORS

The moisture-resistance and decorative potential of tile make it a popular material for use on patios and around swimming pools. Fountains, garden paths, and other walkways are also popular candidates for tiling projects. Until recently, only homeowners in warm climates could consider outdoor tile: Materials and techniques simply were not available to protect tile from cracking under the stress of freeze/thaw conditions. Today, with newer materials and specialized installation procedures (see page 100), tile products can withstand cold temperatures. However, every aspect of the installation must be planned to accommodate freezing conditions. Routine maintenance is critical as well; cracks in the grout or tile should be repaired immediately.

ABOVE: Tile on a pool surround should be set on a concrete pad that is sloped away from the pool for drainage. Use slip-resistant tiles suitable for placement around exterior swimming pools. Installing tile on the inside of a swimming pool is best left to professional tile setters.

LEFT: Stone tiles like the ones on this enclosed patio are ideal for melding indoor and outdoor space. They look great, clean up quickly, and can withstand cold and wet weather. While hearty enough to stand outdoor weather and potted plants, they have a finished beauty that gives this space an almost indoor livability. Decorative ceramic tile on the fountain is an eye-catching feature of the enclosed patio.

PLANNING YOUR TILING PROJECT

The individual elements of good architectural design often go unnoticed. A well-proportioned house or intelligently laid-out kitchen simply has a natural rightness about it. In the same way, instead of shouting for attention, a well-designed tile installation should fit in naturally. When a surfacing material jumps out at you, the design probably has failed.

The age of your house, the decorating style you seek to capture, and your budget all affect the design you choose. Books, magazines, and tile brochures are some of the best sources of ideas. However, be sure the types and patterns of tile that you find attractive suit your space.

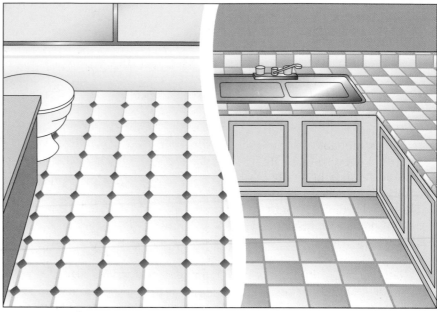

Proportion tile to room size.
As a general rule, tile size should be proportional to the size of the room. That is, small tiles generally work best in small rooms and large tiles look better in large rooms. Larger tiles seem less large when used on horizontal surfaces. Use larger tiles on lower surfaces; wall tiles or countertop tiles that are bigger than the floor tiles tend to make a room top-heavy.

Money $ Saver

OBTAIN DESIGN ADVICE

■ Tile is a permanent surfacing material you'll be living with for a long time to come. It's well worth paying for the advice of an architect or interior decorator if your tiling installation is part of a large remodeling. Other good sources of expertise are flooring retailers and the tiling specialists working at some home centers.

■ Come equipped with dimensions of the space you are tiling and magazine clippings of the styles and materials that you like. Retail specialists may be able to give you all the design guidance you need before launching your project.

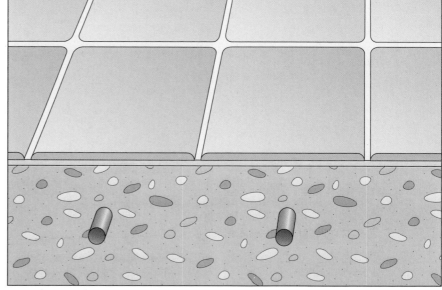

Plan for comfort as well as style.
Radiant heating systems in which heated water passes through tubing embedded in or under the floor surface are becoming increasingly popular. Tile is a great choice for the finish surface on a radiant floor because the tubing usually is embedded in concrete, and a concrete pad is the ideal setting bed for tile. Also, tile is a highly conductive material that conveys heat quickly and efficiently. If you are tiling a new addition or need to improve heating in a room, consider incorporating a radiant heating system into the design.

EXPERTS' INSIGHT

DESIGNING WITH COLOR

With so many stunning tile colors readily available, it's tempting to wield a broad brush and let the color fly. But because today's fashionable color is often tomorrow's eyesore, white and almond tend to be the tones of choice for most homeowners. These light neutral tones help brighten up rooms and can coexist with almost any other color as your decorating schemes change. But many people think too much white or off-white is monotonous. Accent and border colors often cancel out this impression. In rooms with plenty of windows, consider using darker tiles to offset the ambient lighting.

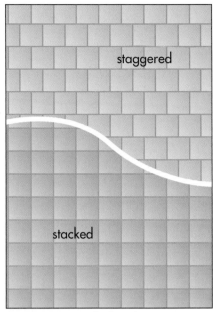

Stagger or stack the tile.
Field tiles usually are installed in a grid pattern or a staggered pattern. A stacked pattern is the easiest, and the clean straight lines appeal to many people. Although they require careful alignment, staggered joints have a pleasingly retro look.

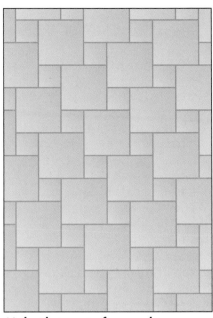

Make the most of one color.
Using only one color of tile does not have to result in a plain-looking installation. Use tiles of different sizes to add a level of contrast. Consider different grout colors and grout joint sizes. Or, use tiles with only small variations in color.

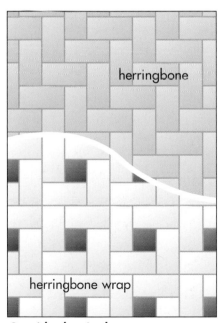

Consider herringbone.
Plain rectangular tiles gain a new dimension when installed in a herringbone pattern. As a variation, wrap a small square tile with rectangular tiles.

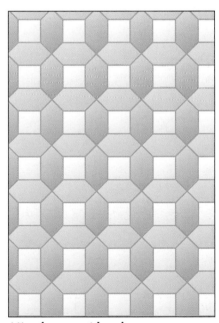

Mix shapes with colors.
Manufacturers offer tiles purposely sized to allow for mixing different shapes into a coherent whole. You can add further interest with this approach by using two or more colors as well.

Define your space.
Borders help define the perimeters of a tile installation and can add a whole new level of interest to the surface. Here, tiles in two colors and a variety of sizes create a border surrounding a field of tiles installed diagonally.

SELECTING THE RIGHT TILE FOR THE JOB

Although simplicity is part of the universal appeal of ceramic tile (it is essentially a thin slab of baked clay), don't assume that just any tile will suit your project. Consider several factors as you select the right tile for the job: the material from which the tile is made (although ceramic tile is made from clay; some tiles do not use clay at all but are actually slabs of stone milled into regular shapes), the degree of firing, the type of glaze, and the shape of the tile, are all factors that affect how and where the tile should be used.

If you are planning several tiling projects for your home, you may want to contact one of the associations created by tile manufacturers, designers, retailers, and installation contractors. These groups have developed standards and acceptable practices relating to tile and tile installations.

The American National Standards Institute (ANSI) has prepared a list of minimum standards that are followed by all professionals in the industry. The Tile Council of America (TCA) publishes the inexpensive annual *Handbook for Ceramic Tile Installation*, which incorporates the ANSI standards. Contact the TCA at P.O. Box 1787, Clemson, SC 29633.

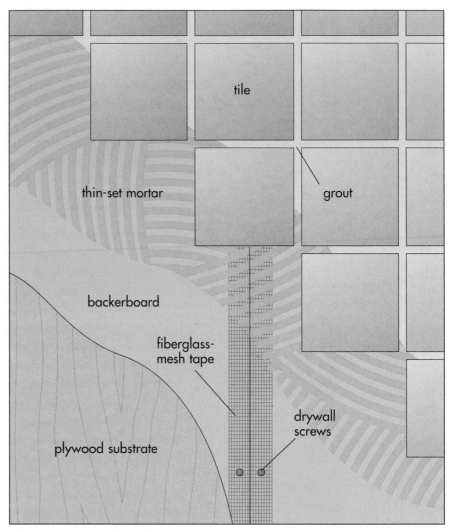

Plan out a typical installation.
Installing tile is a bit like making a sandwich: You proceed one layer at a time. The substrate, often plywood, is the layer in direct contact with the framing (studs for a wall installation or joists for a floor installation). Backerboard serves as the setting bed for the tiles themselves. Adhesives are used to bond each layer. Tiles form the outer layer.

TILE INSTALLATION CHECKLIST

The ANSI standards cover proper materials and installations for just about any type of tile job you can imagine. Use this simple checklist as a design and shopping guide.

Type of Tile	Location of Installation	Special Requirements
☐ glazed wall tile	☐ always dry or limited water exposure	☐ fire resistant
☐ glazed floor tile	☐ frequently wet	☐ stain resistant
☐ ceramic mosaic tile	☐ interior	☐ crack resistant
☐ paver or quarry tile	☐ exterior	☐ color
☐ natural stone	☐ subject to freezing	☐ heavy use

WATER ABSORPTION

Clay absorbs water, and water can cause cracks in tiles and create damage beneath the surface. Ceramic tiles that have been kiln-dried longer and at higher temperatures absorb less water, but they also cost more. So it makes sense to choose tiles precisely rated for the protection you need.

Tile Rating	Best Uses
Nonvitreous	This tile typically is used for decorative purposes only. It is intended for use indoors, in dry locations, such as a fireplace surround or a decorative frieze in a dining room.
Semivitreous	This type of tile is used indoors in dry to occasionally wet locations, such as a kitchen wall or behind a serving area in a dining room.
Vitreous	This multipurpose tile is used indoors or outdoors or in wet or dry locations for anything from bathroom floors or walls to a patio surface.
Impervious	Such tile generally is used only in hospitals, restaurants, and other commercial locations where thorough cleanliness is important.

Choose a glaze.
A glaze is a protective and decorative coating, often colored, that is fired onto the surface of tiles. Glazes can be glossy, matte, or textured. Glazing is not related directly to the water-absorption categories shown above. Although glazing does keep moisture from penetrating the top surface, the unglazed sides and bottoms of the tile don't have the same protection.

EXPERTS' INSIGHT

CHOOSING DECORATIVE TILES

The term *decorative tile* is more descriptive than technical. It broadly defines tiles that have been decorated by molding the clay, handpainting, or affixing a decal to each tile before it is fired. Major tile manufacturers offer a multitude of tiles decorated with flowers, fruits, animals, and other images. Smaller, specialty tile retailers may carry a wider selection of decorative tiles. Individual tilemakers can be a particularly good source of original tiles. (Some will even make tiles to order.) Most decorative tiles are used as accents on walls, backsplashes, and fireplace surrounds.

CAUTION!

THE PERILS OF MIXING TILE
Have you ever run back and forth to the paint store trying to match the color of paint in a new can with the color already on your wall? If so, you'll understand the difficulties of trying to match the colors, and sometimes even the exact sizes, of ceramic tiles. Avoid that aggravation by buying all the tile you think you will need at the same time. Better yet, buy more than you will need; save some of the leftovers for future repairs, and return unopened boxes for a refund.

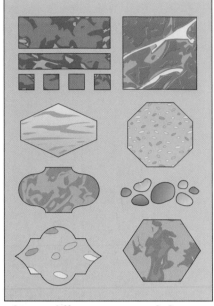

Choose different sizes and shapes.
Square tiles are the most common and the easiest to install. But rectangles, hexagons, and other shapes are available readily. An easy and inexpensive way to add interest to a tile installation is to mix shapes, sizes, and colors; tile retailers and home centers offer a wide range of options.

Select the type of ceramic tile.
Modern ceramic tile is made from refined clay, usually mixed with additives and water. It then is hardened in a kiln. Several different types of tile are created through that process. Quarry tiles are unglazed and vitreous tiles, usually ½ inch thick and used for flooring. Pavers are ⅜-inch-thick vitreous floor tiles and are available glazed or unglazed.

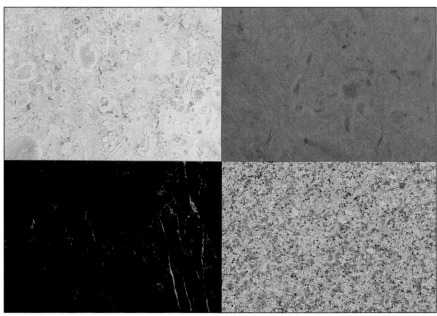

Consider stone tile.
Use natural stone tile on floors, walls, and countertops. Marble, granite, flagstone, and slate are widely available; other types of stone may be available in your area. Dimensioned (or gauged) stone is cut to a uniform size and thickness and can be installed much like ceramic tile. Hand-split (or cleft) stone tiles vary in size and thickness.

EXPERTS' INSIGHT

OTHER TILING CHOICES

Cement-bodied tiles are made with a concrete mix that is extruded or cast, then cured to form a strong, dense tile. They usually are stained to look like pavers, quarry tile, stone, or brick. Often you can buy them with a factory-applied sealer. Brick-veneer tile is made like ceramic tile, but with a coarser body that simulates brick. Terrazzo is manufactured with small pieces of granite or marble set in mortar, then polished. Precast terrazzo tiles are available for floors and walls.

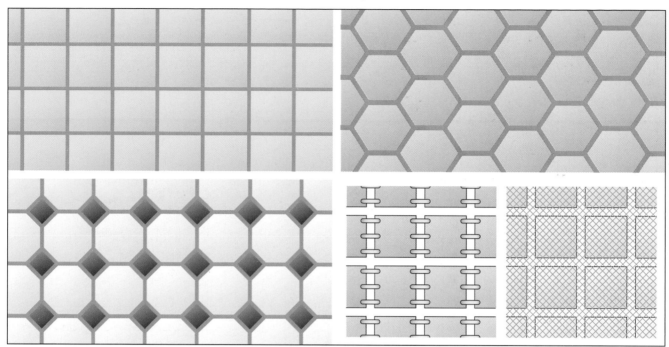

Use mosaic tile.

Mosaic tiles are 1- or 2-inch squares or similarly sized hexagons or pentagons mounted together as a larger unit. Most commercially available mosaics are vitreous and freeze-thaw stable and can be used on most tiling projects. Mosaic tiles are sold almost exclusively mounted on sheets or joined with adhesive strips. Back-mounted mosaic tiles are much easier to install than individual tiles. They can be mounted with standard thin-set mortar and grout.

MEASUREMENTS

NOMINAL VS. ACTUAL SIZE

Most do-it-yourselfers learn quickly that when buying lumber, a 2×4 doesn't measure 2 inches by 4 inches. The tile trade has a similar discrepancy. Individual ceramic tiles are often sold with dimensional names that describe their installed size, that is, the size of the tile plus a standard grout joint. Thus, 6-by-6 inch tiles measure $\frac{1}{8}$ inch shorter in each direction. The actual size will be $5\frac{7}{8}$ by $5\frac{7}{8}$ inches. Only when installed with a $\frac{1}{8}$-inch grout joint will the installed size of the tile be about 6 by 6. Always check the actual size of the tiles before you buy them.

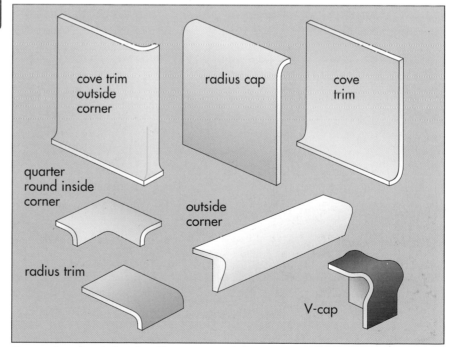

Determine the right trim tiles.

In general, tiles are divided into field tiles, which are flat, and trim tiles, which are shaped irregularly to turn corners or define the edges of an installation. There are dozens of trim-tile profiles, and the names of each can be confusing. When choosing tiles, be sure to check the availability of these specialty tiles and select a style with trim tiles suitable for your project.

SELECTING LAYOUT TOOLS

Layout involves little more than measuring and marking. The tools required are inexpensive hand tools. You probably own most, if not all, of them already.

For making scale drawings, **graph paper** is often the best material to use. You can buy graph paper with various sizes of grids; ¼ inch is the most common. Measure the area to be tiled and sketch it so each ¼-inch grid represent 1 linear foot. The only accessories you will need are a **ruler, pencil,** and **eraser.** Graph paper also comes in handy when sketching tile designs; just let each grid represents a tile.

An **architect's rule** can be used in place of graph paper. An architect's rule has three sides, with different scales marked along each edge. It allows you to quickly convert measured distances to scale, or to count the grids on graph paper. The trick is to choose a scale that will fit on the paper.

A **combination square** or a **framing square** can be used for measuring short distances and precisely marking square corners. You can get by with one or the other, but chances are that you will use both of them if they are available. A framing square also can double as a straightedge to aid in layout and tile installation. Or, you can use short, straight boards, called layout sticks (see right).

A **tape measure** is indispensible for laying out and marking tiles for cutting. You also must have an accurate 2- or 4-foot **level** to check horizontal and vertical surfaces for plumb and to mark accurate layout lines.

An inexpensive **plumb bob** is necessary for finding plumb, and a **chalk line** allows you to quickly mark layout lines. Most chalk lines will perform double duty as plumb bobs. So that you'll be able to clearly see your mark, buy yellow chalk for dark tile and blue chalk for light-colored tile.

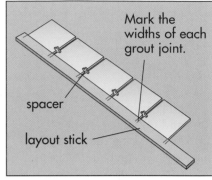

Make a layout stick.
When tiling large, flat surfaces, one of the handiest tools is one you can make yourself. A layout stick is just a homemade ruler that allows you to lay out an installation without having to measure and mark for each tile location. Line up a row of tiles on a flat surface, with spacers between. Set a straight piece of pine alongside the tiles. Start at one end of the stick and mark the width of the grout joint between each tile. You will need a new layout stick if you change tiles or grout widths on a new installation.

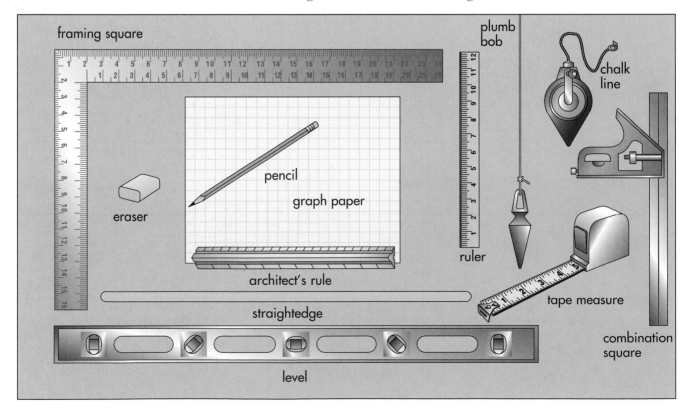

CHOOSING CUTTING TOOLS

One of the goals of setting tile is to lay out the job in a way that minimizes the need to cut tile. But at the very least you will need to cut tiles for corners and around fixtures.

Tile-cutting tools range from the slow and tedious to the fast and furious. Deciding on which tools you need is largely a matter of the size of your project and the number of cuts required.

A **snap cutter** is similar to a hand-held glass cutter, except that it is mounted on a guide bar. Various models operate differently, but all follow a basic two-step approach. First, the tile is set in the cutter and scored along the snap line. Then, the handle is pressed down to snap the tile along the line.

Tile nippers resemble pliers, but they are equipped with carbide-tipped edges. They are indispensable for making small notches and curves in tile. They can also be used for breaking off pieces of tile that have been scored on a snap cutter. Nippers usually leave a rough edge. Use a **rubbing stone** to smooth sharp edges. A **rod saw** blade is a strip of tungsten carbide that fits into a standard **hacksaw** body. It's a slow but handy way to cut tight curves. Another option for making small cuts is a power **diamond-tipped cutter.**

A **wet saw** is a power tool that quickly makes smooth, straight cuts in tile and other masonry. Wet saws are equipped with a pump that sprays water to cool the blade and remove chips. They are messy, but not particularly dangerous or difficult to use. In fact, you might enjoy watching just how easily the blade cuts its way through a piece of tile, marble, or granite.

For drilling holes, use a **carbide-tipped hole saw** mounted on an **electric** or a **cordless power drill.**

> ## CAUTION!
> ### DON'T BUY WHEN YOU CAN RENT
> New home improvement projects offer the perfect excuse to add new tools to your collection. However, some tiling tools are so specialized that you won't use them again until your next tiling job. Buying too many tools can quickly destroy your project budget. Tool-rental stores offer a variety of tools, many specifically chosen for do-it-yourselfers needing special tools for a short period of time. For tiling projects, it's especially smart to rent power tools, such as a wet saw or a diamond-tipped cutter. Also, check with your tile supplier. Often the store will lend customers tools at no charge if the tiles were purchased there.

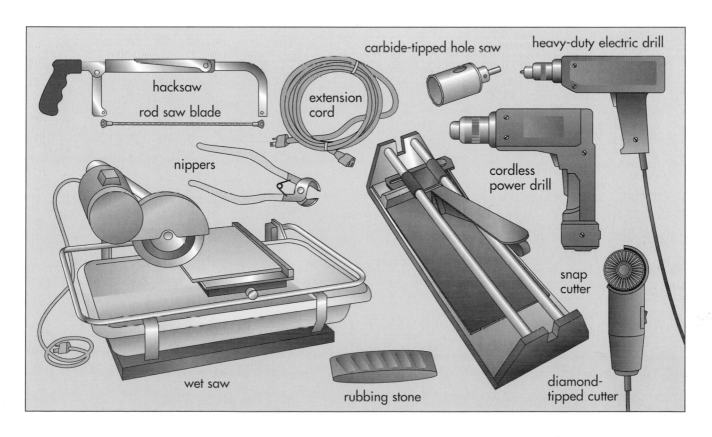

hacksaw

rod saw blade

carbide-tipped hole saw

heavy-duty electric drill

extension cord

nippers

cordless power drill

wet saw

rubbing stone

snap cutter

diamond-tipped cutter

SELECTING INSTALLATION TOOLS

For mixing thin-set mortar and grout, you need a sturdy bucket. An empty, clean **drywall-compound bucket** will suffice for relatively small jobs, but a **mortar-mixing box** is better for larger jobs. A **mortar mixer** is a great time saver for mixing two or more gallons of thin-set mortar or grout. The mixer is mounted, like a drill bit, on an electric drill.

Notched trowels have two smooth sides for spreading adhesive and two notched sides for combing the adhesive to the right depth. Check the tile and adhesive manufacturers' recommendations for the proper notch size.

You'll need a **beating block** to press the tiles evenly into the adhesive. Use a piece of 2× lumber covered with terry cloth or buy a rubber-faced model. With Mexican pavers and other irregular tiles, use a **rubber mallet** instead.

A canvas **drop cloth** readily absorbs moisture and has enough heft to protect surfaces from dropped tiles. Use **masking tape** to cover plumbing fixtures.

CAUTION!
SAFETY EQUIPMENT
Installing tile is not a particularly dangerous occupation, especially if you exercise common sense and follow a few basic safety practices. When using power tools or cutting tile with hand tools, protect your eyes with safety goggles. Plug power tools into an outlet or extension cord equipped with a ground-fault circuit interrupter (GFCI). When mixing and handling adhesive and grout, wear a charcoal-filter mask and rubber gloves.

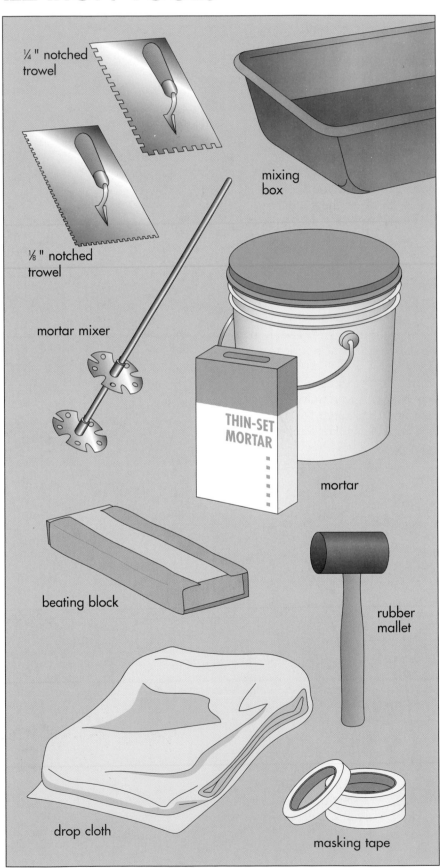

¼" notched trowel

⅛" notched trowel

mixing box

mortar mixer

THIN-SET MORTAR

mortar

beating block

rubber mallet

drop cloth

masking tape

CHOOSING GROUTING TOOLS

Many of the tools used for applying thin-set mortar also can be used for spreading grout. A **grouting float** is a rubber-backed trowel used for pressing the grout into the joints. It also removes excess grout from the tiling surface, although a **squeegee** may be more thorough. A **mason's trowel** is handy for finishing grout joints, although you also can use a **putty knife** or the handle of an **old toothbrush**. A **margin trowel** is used to mix small batches and to scoop adhesive or grout onto the setting surface. A **grout bag** is useful when you need to force grout into joints that can't be reached easily with a grout float.

Good-quality **sponges** are best for cleaning grout off the tile surface. Look for sponges made especially for tiling work. Use **cheesecloth** to remove the haze left on the tile after the grout has set for a while. For applying caulk and sealant around edges, you will need a **caulking gun**.

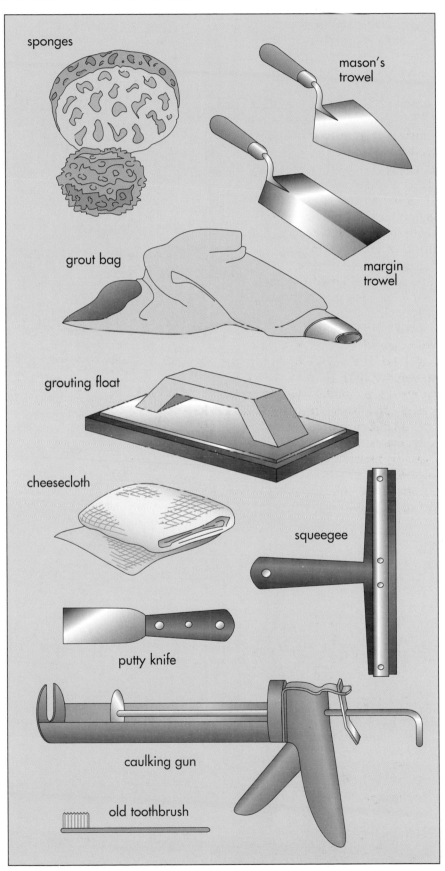

sponges

mason's trowel

grout bag

margin trowel

grouting float

cheesecloth

squeegee

putty knife

caulking gun

old toothbrush

USING TILE SPACERS

The space between tiles serves two important functions: It provides room for the grout essential to any tile job, and it allows for some creativity in your design. You can change the look of a finished tile installation significantly by changing the width of the grout joint or by altering the color of the grout.

Tile spacers are small pieces of plastic used to ensure consistent width of the grout joints. They come in a variety of sizes and shapes to match different types of tile and tile installations. Many types of ceramic tile today are *self-spacing*; that is, they have small lugs along their sides that ensure proper spacing. If you use self-spacing tiles, you need not use tile spacers unless you prefer a wider grout joint than the lugs allow.

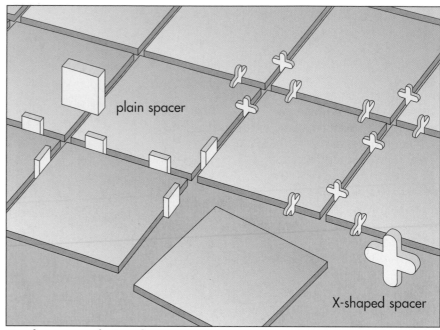

Purchase manufactured spacers.
Buy plastic tile spacers from your tile supplier. They are available in sizes from $\frac{1}{16}$ inch to $\frac{1}{2}$ inch. X-shaped spacers are the most common. They are placed in or around each corner. Though less common, plain spacers often are preferred for spacing and holding wall tiles firmly in place.

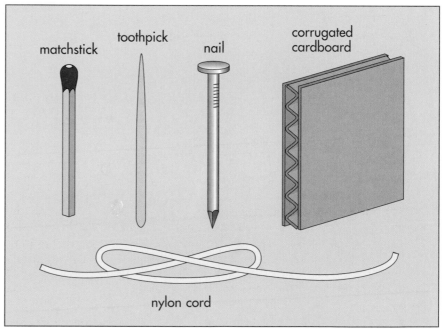

Make your own spacers.
Plastic spacers are one of the least expensive materials used for tile installation. But for a small job or in a pinch, you may need to resort to an alternative. Look for objects that have a consistent size, such as wooden matchsticks, toothpicks, or nails. Nylon cord can be used for a long run. Remember to remove the spacers before grouting.

SELECTING ADHESIVES

The setting adhesive bonds the bottom of the tile with the setting bed. Recent improvements in setting adhesives make it easy for do-it-yourselfers to set tile with professional results. Although adhesives fall into the broad categories of organic mastic and thin-set mortar, in reality there are many types of products and manufacturers. The first step in choosing an adhesive is to determine what kind of installation you are doing (wet or dry? indoor or outdoor? floor or wall?) and to what substrate the tile will be applied.

Organic mastics are popular because they require no mixing. However, they are not suitable for areas exposed to heat or for exterior installations. Thin-set mortars usually are mixed by the installer. A variety of thin-set additives are available to create an adhesive best suited to specific installations. The chart below offers general guidelines.

Buy ready-mixed organic mastic.
Organic mastic is a premixed adhesive that is easy to use. It is especially popular for use on walls because tiles will not slip when set in place.

Mix your own thin-set mortar.
Thin-set mortar requires more work than does organic mastic, but offers superior bonding strength and flexibility.

CHOOSING THIN-SET MORTARS	
Type	**Description and Uses**
Water-mixed mortar	Also referred to as *dry-set mortar,* this is a blend of portland cement, sand, and additives. Mix with water.
Latex- and acrylic-mixed mortar	Also referred to as *latex mortar,* this mortar is similar to water-mixed mortar, but has latex or acrylic added to it. The additives improve adhesion and reduce water absorption; they may be premixed with the mortar in dry form or added as a liquid by the installer. It's an excellent choice for both wet and dry installations.
Epoxy mortar	This is a mixture of sand, cement, and liquid resins and hardeners. It's costly, but effective with any setting material and is a good choice when the substrate is incompatible with other adhesives.
Medium-bed mortar	This adhesive remains stronger than regular thin-set mortar when applied in layers of more than ¼ inch. It's useful with tiles that do not have uniform backs, such as handmade tiles and ungauged stone.

CHOOSING SETTING BEDS

A tile installation is only as good as the surface to which it is applied. Investing in adequate materials for the setting bed is as important as buying the right tile for your project. Tiled floors, in particular, require an extremely stiff setting bed; any imperfection in the subfloor can crack tiles and ruin your project.

You may be able to set the tile over an existing subfloor or wall surface, or you may want to add a layer or two of setting material to ensure a stiff and durable installation. The introduction of cement-based and gypsum-based backerboard has dramatically simplified tile installations without compromising strength and durability. Previously, tile was applied over thick beds of mortar, almost exclusively by trained professionals. The process was time-consuming and required skill and experience.

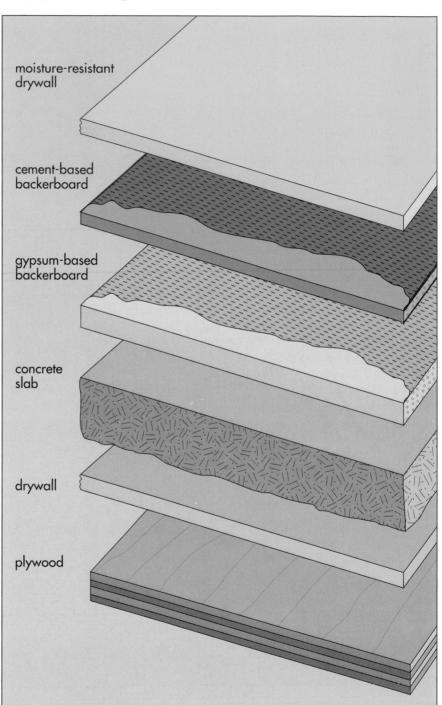

EXPERTS' INSIGHT

MORTAR-BED INSTALLATIONS

Modern thin-set mortars are typically applied in a layer only 1/8- to 1/4-inch thick; that's how they get their name. Traditional (mudset) tile installations use thick mortar as the setting bed. Mortar, with wire-mesh reinforcement, is poured over tar paper to a thickness of 1 to 2 inches. Then the tiles are set on the mortar before it cures. Mortar-bed installations are strong and particularly useful on shower floors.

Choose a setting bed.
Drywall (regular or moisture-resistant) is a suitable setting bed only in dry areas; for a stronger setting bed, use two layers. Backerboard often is called cement board, although some products contain no cement. Sold in varying thicknesses and sizes, backerboard is easy to install and provides a ready-made surface for setting tile. Cement-based backerboard has a mesh coat and is cut using a carbide-tipped scoring tool. Gypsum-based backerboard can be cut with a utility knife.

Concrete slabs (old or newly poured) are ideal setting beds for tile floors. With suitable adhesives, tile can be installed over plywood.

Labels in illustration: moisture-resistant drywall, cement-based backerboard, gypsum-based backerboard, concrete slab, drywall, plywood

SELECTING GROUT

Grout is a mortar used to fill the joints between tiles. It stiffens the tile installation and helps prevent moisture from penetrating the joint. Grout usually is sold with all of the dry ingredients mixed together; the installer adds the liquid. It is also available in caulking-gun and squeeze tubes with the wet and dry ingredients already mixed and ready for application.

Grout not only seals joints, it plays an important role in the overall design. The width and color of the grout joint can radically alter the finished look of a tile installation. Choose a grout color to complement, match, or contrast with the tile. Increase or decrease the joint size to provide the most appropriate balance based on the room's size.

CHOOSING GROUT

Type	Description and Uses
Plain grout	Also referred to as unsanded grout, it is a mixture of Portland cement and additives chosen to achieve specific characteristics. It is used for grout joints of 1/16 inch or less. It's also recommended for absorptive tile and marble.
Sanded grout	This is similar to plain grout, but has sand added. It is used for grout joints greater than 1/16 inch. The ratio between sand and cement varies, depending on the size of the joint.
Epoxy grout	This grout contains epoxy resin and hardener. It's used when chemical and stain resistance are required or where high temperatures are likely.
Colored grout	Offered in premixed packages in a wide assortment of colors and formulations, a colored grout will match almost any need and fill any typical grout joint. Natural grout can be used if you prefer the look of cement.
Mortar	This is similar to sanded grout, but is used for joints between brick pavers, slate, or other masonry materials.
Premixed grout	Some grouts are available premixed and ready to use out of the container. Choices are fewer, and the cost is high, but it may be a good choice for small jobs.

Know your grout.
Grout and tile are the two visible materials on a tiled surface. A good tile installation requires a good grouting job. Use the best ingredients, mix them right, and apply the grout so it completely fills the joints between tiles. Although tile is completely inflexible, you can achieve some flexibility in the grout joints by adding latex or acrylic additives to the grout. Additives also can increase water and stain resistance. When grout joints begin to fail, they should be repaired immediately or water damage could occur behind the tile.

SELECTING MEMBRANES

In addition to backerboard or other bed materials (page 24), some installations call for use of a membrane. The two types are waterproofing membranes and isolation membranes.

Waterproofing membranes are used to prevent moisture from penetrating through the surface (usually the grout joint). If water will often sit on your floor tiles, or if your wall tiles will be in a room that often becomes very humid, moisture can seep through grout or unglazed tiles and cause serious damage to the substrate and even the structural wood. A sealer (page 27) may solve the problem for wall tiles, but floor tiles that will get soaked need a membrane.

Tar paper (that is, felt paper saturated with tar) has long been the standard waterproofing membrane. Polyethylene sheeting is another inexpensive option. The most effective waterproofing membrane is chlorinated

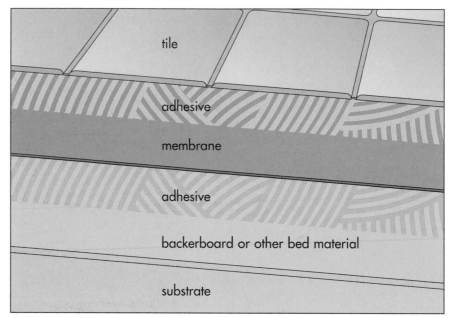

polyethylene (CPE), a strong and thick sheet that is joined to the substrate with adhesive. Liquid membranes are applied with trowel or brush.

The function of an isolation membrane is to protect the tiled surface from damage due to

movement in the underlying surface. Use one when you tile over an existing floor that shows signs of movement from seasonal changes or settling of the house. Chlorinated polyethylene sheets are often used as isolation membranes.

Tar paper waterproofing.
Tar paper is an inexpensive and easy-to-install membrane. It is sold in rolls of varying widths and lengths, and can be stapled or nailed to studs or drywall.

CPE waterproofing.
Chlorinated polyethylene is a durable and flexible product that offers the best water resistance of any available membrane. It is particularly effective on floors that will be wet on a regular basis.

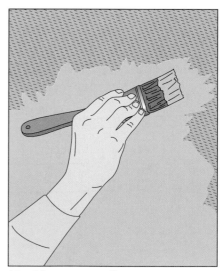

Liquid waterproofing.
Single-component liquid membranes are spread on the setting bed. Once cured, they form a reasonably waterproof layer. Multicomponent membranes require liquid and fabric installed in layers.

CHOOSING CAULK AND SEALERS

Tiles may last centuries, but a tile installation has no chance of reaching such a ripe old age unless it is well maintained. Some components of the installation need to be replaced or renewed every few years. *Caulk* refers to a variety of flexible products used to fill joints that should not be grouted for one reason or another. *Sealers* are protective coatings applied over the entire tiled surface or all the grout lines; they prevent staining and protect tile and grout from water infiltration.

The best choice for a long-lasting, mildew-free joint in high-moisture installations is silicone caulk. Latex caulk is not suitable for tile jobs. Use siliconized acrylic caulk in areas exposed to only minimal moisture. Tub-and-tile caulk contains a mildewcide, but isn't always effective in completely preventing mildew.

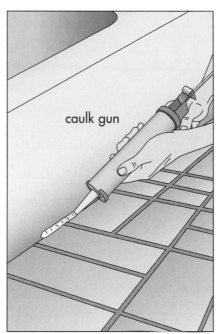

Where to caulk.
Use caulk instead of grout in expansion joints (see box below), between dissimilar materials, and around penetrations in the tiled surface such as between tiles and a

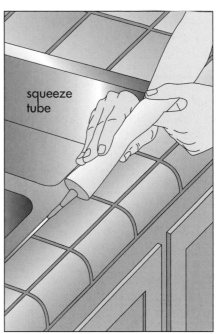

sink. Like grout, caulk is available in sanded and plain formulations, and in colors that match the grout. Caulk tubes used with a caulk gun are the easiest to use. Buy a squeeze tube for small jobs.

TILE AND GROUT SEALERS

Sealers are used on unglazed tile and stone products. They are also applied to grout. *Penetrating sealers* are intended to be absorbed beneath the surface of the tile and grout. They reduce the absorbency of the surface without necessarily adding a sheen. *Coating sealers* are formulated to remain on the surface, where they generally add a glossy or semigloss sheen. Use a *grout sealer* on a wall with glazed tile. It will keep your grout watertight and make it easier to clean. Usually, you must wait two weeks after tile installation before applying grout sealer.

EXPERTS' INSIGHT

EXPANSION JOINTS

■ Tile and grout generally don't expand and contract with seasonal and temperature changes, but the materials beneath and around them may. Expansion joints are safety features that anticipate that movement and prevent the tile and grout from being damaged by it. On most installations, expansion joints are intended to look like grout joints, but they are filled with a flexible material such as silicone caulk.

■ Use expansion joints around the perimeters of all tile installations, especially where the tile edges meet a different material. Use them where floors meet walls, countertops meet backsplashes, and where tile meets wood or another material. Any runs of tile on a floor that exceed 24 feet must be interrupted with an expansion joint.

■ The most typical method of creating an expansion gap is to leave a $\frac{1}{4}$-inch joint between the tile and the adjoining surface, then fill the joint with caulk. The setting bed should also be designed with expansion joints.

ASSESSING SUBSTRATES

The *substrate* of a floor or wall includes the setting bed (page 24) and any other layers beneath the tile surface. Even if tile adheres firmly to its setting bed, it won't last long if that setting bed isn't part of a completely sound and sturdy substrate.

The structural needs of your substrate may change when you add a new type of surface. For example, if you are planning to install ceramic tile on a floor that currently is covered with resilient sheet flooring, you will be adding a lot of weight to the underlying framing. If you doubt that the joists and subfloor are strong enough, consult a professional.

A quick way to tell if a floor is firm enough to handle ceramic tile: Jump on it. If it feels springy, there's a good chance that your tiles or grout lines will crack in time. Add a layer of plywood or backerboard to strengthen it, or consult a professional to be sure.

Walls should be firm to the touch. New tiles will not add significant strength.

SUBSTRATE RECOMMENDATIONS

Substrate	Preparation
Exposed joists	■ Verify that the framing will support the new floor. ■ Install ¾-inch CDX (structural) plywood. ■ Install backerboard or underlayment-grade plywood.
Concrete slab	■ Repair cracks or low spots in the concrete. ■ Ensure that the slab is flat, clean, and dry. ■ Roughen the surface to improve adhesion.
Finished floor	■ Verify that the framing will support the new floor. ■ If necessary, remove the finished flooring. ■ Install backerboard or underlayment-grade plywood over suitable subfloor, or over the finished flooring.
Wall paneling	■ Remove thin sheet paneling. ■ Install backerboard, plywood, or drywall.
Drywall	■ Scrape away any loose paint and roughen the surface with sandpaper. ■ Clean the surface, or apply deglosser. ■ Add a second layer of drywall for added strength.
Masonry or plaster walls	■ Repair cracks and level indentations. ■ Ensure that the surface is sound, not soft and crumbling or springy when pressed. ■ Clean the surface, or apply deglosser.

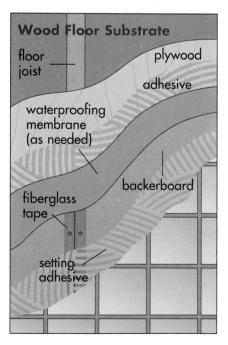

Wood Floor Substrate

floor joist

plywood

adhesive

waterproofing membrane (as needed)

backerboard

fiberglass tape

setting adhesive

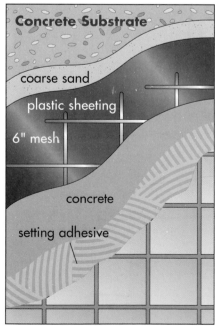

Concrete Substrate

coarse sand

plastic sheeting

6" mesh

concrete

setting adhesive

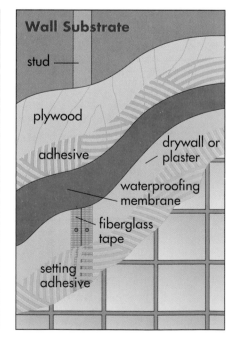

Wall Substrate

stud

plywood

adhesive

drywall or plaster

waterproofing membrane

fiberglass tape

setting adhesive

CALCULATING MATERIALS

Before you go shopping for tile and related materials, determine how much of each material you need. Fortunately, that doesn't mean that you have to count every last tile you intend to install. Tiling materials are usually sold by the square foot—so for most jobs, all you have to do is measure the surface to be tiled, then take that number to the store with you.

Buy more tile than you plan to use. Expect to break a few tiles and to need a few more than anticipated. It's handy to have a few extra tiles should you need to replace any tiles later, so get 5 to 10 percent more than your estimate.

Where to Buy

Tile and setting materials are widely available. Small lumber yards and hardware stores may carry a limited selection, while home centers and tile outlets offer a much wider choice. It pays to shop around because prices and selection can vary significantly. Of course you should shop for a good price, but also look for a retailer who is knowledgeable and willing to answer questions. A little good advice might save you plenty of time and money. Be sure to ask about the store's policy on returns. In the event that you buy considerably more than you need, you should be able to return unopened boxes and packages for a refund.

Metrics

Tiles are manufactured and sold all over the world. So the tiles you choose may have been manufactured to a metric size, which was then rounded off to inches. So, for example, you may have a "13-inch" Italian tile that actually measures $13\frac{3}{16}$ inches.

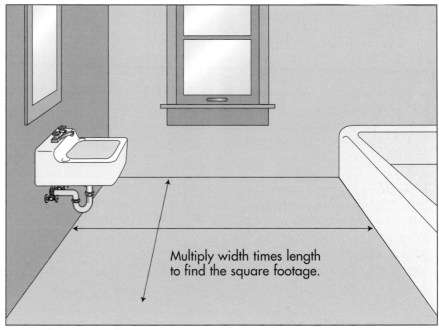

Multiply width times length to find the square footage.

Determine square footage.
If you are tiling a single rectangular surface, simply measure the width and the length (in feet), and multiply the two numbers to determine the square footage. For multiple surfaces, calculate each one separately, then add the results. For walls with a door or a window, include the obstruction in your initial calculation, then calculate the square footage of the obstruction and subtract it from the total.

If you will be installing large, expensive tiles, make a drawing of your space (with exact dimensions) and bring it to your dealer, who can help you to determine the most economical layout.

ESTIMATING GROUT AND ADHESIVES

The amount of grout you need depends on the size of the tiles and on the width and depth of the grout joint. Packages of grout often include tables for estimating the amount needed. This chart gives you a rough idea of how many square feet can be covered with one pound of grout. The figures should be treated only as estimates, but they do show how much the coverage changes depending on tile size.

Tile Size	Joint Width	Coverage per Pound of Grout
2"×2"×$\frac{1}{4}$"	$\frac{1}{16}$"	24 square feet
$4\frac{1}{4}$"×$4\frac{1}{4}$"×$\frac{5}{16}$"	$\frac{1}{16}$"	16 square feet
$4\frac{1}{4}$"×$4\frac{1}{4}$"×$\frac{5}{16}$"	$\frac{1}{8}$"	8 square feet
6"×6"×$\frac{1}{4}$"	$\frac{1}{16}$"	28 square feet
6"×6"×$\frac{1}{4}$"	$\frac{1}{8}$"	14 square feet
12"×12"×$\frac{3}{8}$"	$\frac{1}{16}$"	37 square feet

When applied with the trowel notch size recommended by the manufacturer, one gallon of adhesive will cover 30–50 square feet of wall and 20–40 square feet of floor.

PREPARING THE SITE

When tiling floors or installing wall tiles down to the floor line, remove baseboard trim. If the baseboard is trimmed with shoe molding (a thin rounded strip attached to the floor), you probably need only remove the shoe, leaving the baseboard in place, in order to tile the floor. If you plan to reuse the trim, take care not to damage it as you remove it. Insert a thin pry bar or stiff putty knife to lift the shoe or pull the baseboard from the wall. Gradually work your way along the molding until it comes off. Write numbers on the backs of the pieces to help you remember where they go. Remove as many obstacles as possible so you will not have to make many precise tile cuts. When preparing to tile a floor, set a tile on the floor and use it as a guide for cutting the bottoms of casing molding.

If you are tiling a bathroom, remember that removing and replacing a toilet is easier than tiling around it, and will lead to a much cleaner-looking job. (Be sure to stuff a rag in the soil pipe to prevent sewer gas from backing up

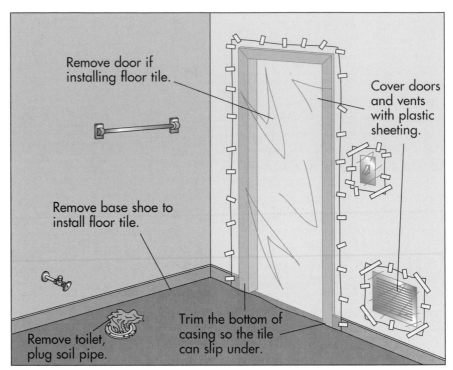

Remove door if installing floor tile.

Cover doors and vents with plastic sheeting.

Remove base shoe to install floor tile.

Remove toilet, plug soil pipe.

Trim the bottom of casing so the tile can slip under.

into the bathroom.) You may want to remove the vanity as well as doors. (You may also need to trim the doors after the tile is installed.)

When preparing to tile walls, remove electrical outlet covers (the outlet box may have to be adjusted before replacing the covers), and fixtures. Sinks and appliances may have to be

removed, depending on your installation. Because the tiles add thickness to the wall, it is usually best to leave window and door casings in place. Keep dust and odors from spreading throughout the house by taping plastic sheeting over doorways. Cover vents with plastic as well.

PREPARING SURFACES TO BE TILED

Floors
■ Remove the original flooring, if it is not firmly stuck to the subfloor, if it is uneven, or if the thinset mortar will not adhere to it.
■ Make sure that the subfloor is at least $1\frac{1}{8}$ inch thick and composed of suitable materials (usually a combination of plywood, backerboard, or concrete).
■ If a plywood floor seems loose in spots, drive nails or screws through it into floor joists.
■ Fill low spots in the subfloor, then smooth the surface and clean it thoroughly.

Walls
■ Remove wallpaper, thin paneling, or anything else that flexes when you press it.
■ When tiling over new drywall, don't bother taping the joints but do seal the surface with a thin coat of adhesive applied with the flat side of a trowel.
■ Scrape away loose paint.
■ Lightly sand glossy surfaces to remove the sheen.
■ Patch holes and cracks, and sand smooth.
■ Thoroughly clean the wall and allow it to dry.

Countertops
■ Remove sink or faucets, and other obstacles.
■ Remove any existing tile.
■ To tile over a square-edged laminated countertop that is sound, give it a thorough sanding and remove the backsplash.
■ If you have a post-form countertop with curved edges, remove it and install a new substrate of plywood and backerboard.
■ Make sure the substrate is thick enough for trim pieces, and that the trim won't prevent drawers from opening.

LAYING OUT THE JOB

*T*ile looks best when it is set in a straight line, and at least appears to be square and level with adjacent surfaces. Laying out the installation is the most important step for ensuring such an outcome. Tile is an unforgiving material, and floors and walls are rarely as square and level as you might think—or hope. One of the secrets to a successful layout, therefore, is learning how to fudge the installation so the fudging isn't apparent. The other secret is to plan for as few cut tiles as possible. Adjust the layout to minimize cuts, and hide those cut tiles along less conspicuous walls and under baseboard trim. Don't be surprised if your house exceeds some of the tolerances recommended here. Tile setters have had to deal with such irregularities for centuries.

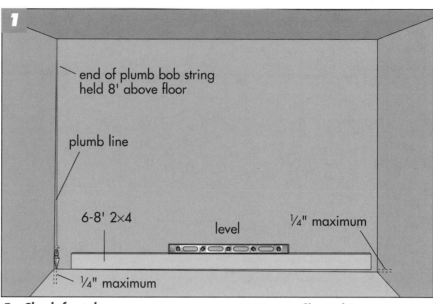

end of plumb bob string held 8' above floor

plumb line

6-8' 2×4

level

¼" maximum

¼" maximum

1. Check for tolerances.
Check tiling surfaces for square, level, and plumb using the techniques shown below. If a surface is out of alignment more than the amounts shown above, the best solution is to adjust the surfaces—for instance, add furring strips to a wall, or shim up a subfloor. If this is not feasible, make the unevenness less visible by avoiding narrow tile pieces at the corner. You might be able to split the difference, making two edges slightly out of line instead of having one edge that is way off.

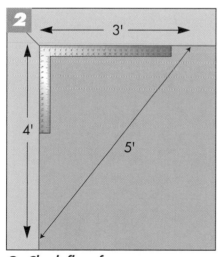

3'

4'

5'

2. Check floor for square.
For small rooms, check the squareness of the floor by setting a framing square at inside and outside corners. For larger rooms, use the 3-4-5 method: Measure along one wall exactly 3 feet from the corner, and along the other wall 4 feet. If the distance between those spots is exactly 5 feet, the floor is square.

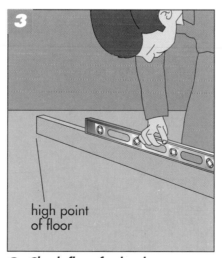

high point of floor

3. Check floor for level.
Use a 2- or 4-foot level to check along each wall. To check for level over a longer span, place the level on the edge of a straight 6- or 8-foot board. If the floor is only slightly out of level, and you are not planning to run tile up the wall, this should not affect your installation.

Bubble indicates level.

4. Check walls for plumb.
Place a level vertically on the wall at various spots, or use a plumb bob. Set the level horizontally on the wall to see how flat it is (you can also stretch a string tightly along the wall). A wavy wall, even if it is plumb, should be corrected before tiling.

EXPERTS' INSIGHT

PLANNING FOR FOCAL POINTS

When you walk into a room for the first time, chances are there is something that catches your eye immediately. As you stand in the room, other areas may become more noticeable. It might be another doorway, a fireplace, a window, counters, or appliance groupings. Plan your layout so that the installation looks best in these focal areas. Cut tiles placed around a sink should all be of equal size, for example. If your floor is out of square so that you must have a line of cut tiles that grows progressively smaller, plan ahead so it will be behind a couch or in an area that is not a focal point. Use perpendicular lines and full tiles at focal points.

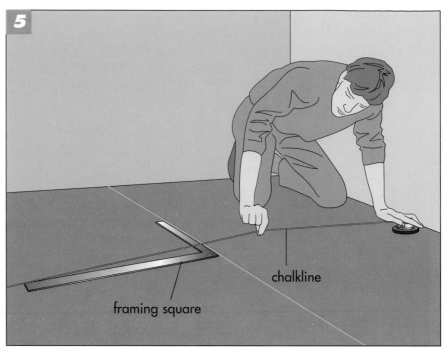

chalkline

framing square

5. Establish reference lines.
Accurate reference lines are critical to the success of a tile installation. Trace around a piece of plywood with two factory edges, or chalk two lines that are perfectly perpendicular. You will place the first tile at the intersection; this tile establishes the alignment and position of the rest of the tiles. (For more instruction and information about tiling specific areas, see the Tiling Projects section, pages 52-103.)

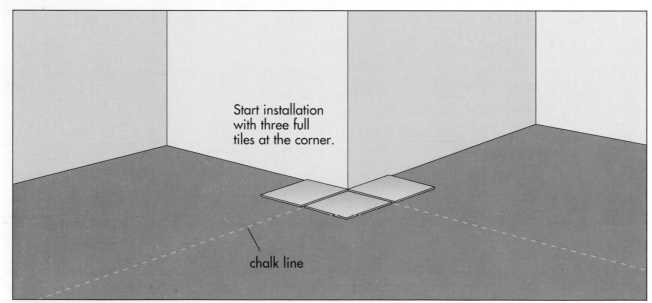

Start installation with three full tiles at the corner.

chalk line

Laying out an L-shaped room.
Often, the outside corner of an L-shaped room will be a focal point, so start there. Here's the simplest way to lay it out: From the corner, extend two straight lines along the floor to the opposing wall. Plan to set three full tiles at the corner, then extend the layout. However, this will not work if the outside corner is seriously out of square. Also, if this method results in very small pieces along a wall, it may be best to modify it.

6. Do a dry run.

With reference lines drawn, you can measure from the lines to the walls and calculate how the tiles will be arranged. However, the safest method is to set tiles in place along the reference lines.

For this dry run, don't use any adhesive, but be sure to space the tiles properly. Take your time, and find out how each edge will look. Don't hesitate to change the entire layout if it will make for a more attractive appearance.

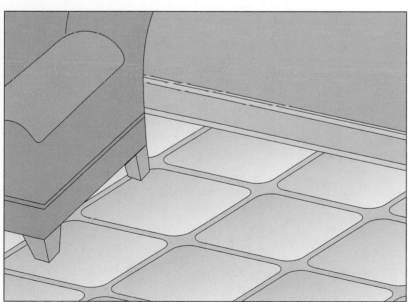

Hiding cut tiles.

One big advantage of a careful and thorough layout is that you can plan where cut tiles will go. A simple rule of thumb is to place cut tiles in the least visible areas. On a floor installation, for example, one wall may be largely covered with furniture. If you place cut tiles under the furniture, they are not likely to be seen. On other installations, you may prefer to adjust the layout so that it has evenly sized cut tiles along the opposing surfaces.

Money $ Saver

USING TILE SCRAPS

By making adjustments in your layout, you can save some money. That's because you can plan ahead to use as many of your tile cutoffs as possible. As explained below, avoid using tiles that are less than half size. There are times when you won't have a choice, however, especially if you are tiling an oddly shaped room or an irregular surface. In those cases, try to use tiles that have already been cut rather than wasting full ones. Tile scraps can also be used for mosaic installations.

CAUTION!
AVOID NARROW TILES

One of the golden rules of tile setting is to use as many full tiles as possible. Another rule is to avoid using tiles that have been cut in size by more than half. Sometimes those rules are easier to remember than to follow. Then, follow the most important rule: Avoid using very narrow tiles. Not only are they unattractive, but they may not adhere properly. When your layout reveals the need for one row of very narrow tiles, make an adjustment. Plan to cut tiles along two rows rather than one; that way they won't be so narrow.

CUTTING WITH A CIRCULAR SAW

Whether crosscutting 2×4s, ripping plywood, or cutting tiles or bricks with a masonry blade, you'll do the job better if you follow a few basic rules for using a circular saw.

Whenever you cut, allow the saw to reach full operating speed, then slowly push the blade into the wood. Some carpenters look at the blade as they cut; others rely on the gunsight notch. Choose the method that suits you best. Avoid making slight turns as you cut. Find the right path, and push the saw through the material smoothly. It will take some practice before you can do this consistently. This is a powerful tool with sharp teeth, so take care. It demands your respect. Support the material to avoid having the saw bind and possibly kick back at you. Don't wear loose-fitting long sleeves or position your face near the blade.

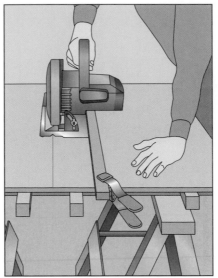

Support the material properly.
A well-supported board results in clean, safe cuts. If the scrap piece is short, support the board on the nonscrap side. If the scrap is long, it could bind the blade or splinter as it falls away at the end of the cut, so support it in four places.

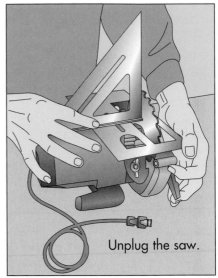

Unplug the saw.

Square the blade.
Turn the saw upside down, hold a square against the blade, and adjust it. (Be sure to position the square between the teeth.) Cut some scrap pieces and check to make sure the saw cuts squarely through the thickness of the board.

TOOLS TO USE

CIRCULAR SAW AND BLADES

■ Choose a circular saw that is comfortable. It should have some heft, but should not be so heavy that it is difficult to maneuver. You should be able to see the blade and gunsight notch easily. Check for ease of depth and angle adjustments.

■ If you buy only one blade for cutting lumber and plywood, chose a carbide-tipped combination blade that has at least 24 teeth. It works well for rough work and makes cuts clean enough for most finish work. For more specialized uses, buy a plywood blade, a finishing blade, or a masonry blade.

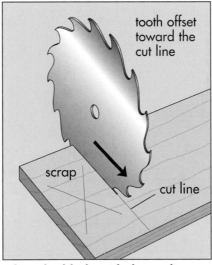

tooth offset toward the cut line

scrap

cut line

Align the blade with the cut line.
Once you have drawn an accurate cutoff line and have properly supported the board, position the saw blade on the scrap side of the line. The teeth on most blades are offset in an alternating pattern. When preparing to cut, look at a tooth that points toward the cutoff line.

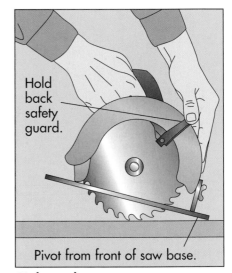

Hold back safety guard.

Pivot from front of saw base.

Make a plunge cut.
Use a plunge cut, also called a pocket cut, to make a hole or slit in the middle of a board or sheet. Set the blade to the correct depth. Retract the safety guard and tilt the saw forward, setting the front of the baseplate on the stock. Start the saw and lower it slowly into the cut line until the base rests on the stock. Complete the cut.

DRILLING

An electric drill enables you not only to drill a hole of almost any size with ease, but also to drive screws into wood or metal, buff and grind, and even mix mortar or paint.

Many craftsmen keep two drills on hand—one for drilling pilot holes and the other for driving screws. That way, they don't waste time changing bits. A drill with a keyless chuck speeds up a bit change, although you may find that bits slip during heavy-duty tasks.

In addition to the bits shown at right, purchase a magnetic sleeve that holds inexpensive screwdriver bits. This simple tool will make driving screws nearly as easy as pounding nails.

EXPERTS' INSIGHT

CHOOSING A DRILL

■ Avoid buying a cheap drill with a ¼-inch chuck. It will not have the power you need and will soon burn out. A good drill will be variable-speed and reversing (VSR), will have a ⅜-inch chuck, and will pull at least 3 amps. One tipoff to a better-quality tool is the cord. Look for a long cord that flexes more like rubber than plastic.

■ Choose a heavy-duty, ½-inch drill if you will be using it to mix mortar. A smaller drill can burn out quickly while churning this thick substance.

■ A cordless drill can make your work go more easily, but only if it is powerful enough to do most things that a corded drill can do.

■ A hammer drill is useful if you need to drill a number of holes in concrete.

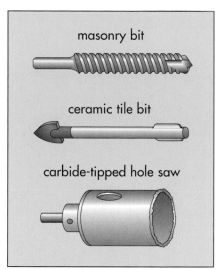

Choose the right bit.
Use standard twist or spade bits for boring through wood. A carbide-tipped masonry bit drills through concrete or brick. Use a carbide-tipped hole saw for larger holes. A ceramic tile bit will make a hole in tile without cracking it.

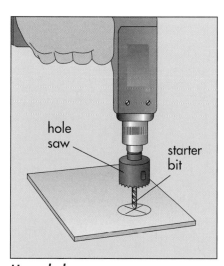

Use a hole saw.
Cutting a hole in the middle of a tile is easy to do with a carbide-tipped hole saw. Measure to the center of the hole (you will need to make two measurements), and place the tile on a flat surface that you don't mind damaging. Nick the center point to keep the starter bit from wandering. Keep the drill perpendicular in both directions as you drill, and don't press too hard.

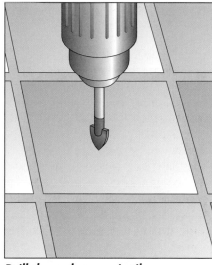

Drill through ceramic tile.
Wall tiles are usually soft, but floor tiles can be very tough. Nick the surface of the tile just enough so the bit will not wander as you drill. Keep the bit and the hole lubricated with a few drops of oil. Use a masonry bit or ceramic tile bit like the one shown above.

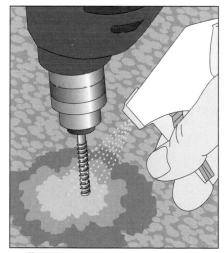

Drill into masonry and concrete.
Use a masonry bit when drilling masonry surfaces. Usually, brick is easy to drill into and concrete is more difficult. Check the bit often to make sure it's not overheating. Stop if you see smoke. Spraying the bit with window cleaner as you work keeps the bit cool, and the foaming action brings debris up and out of the hole.

CUTTING BACKERBOARD

Backerboard usually has to be cut to size before it can be installed. You may also have to drill holes in the board so that it will slide into place. If you have ever installed drywall, you will find the score-and-snap method to be very familiar. There are several types of backerboard on the market, and new materials are introduced from time to time. Be sure to follow the manufacturer's instructions if they vary from the process described here. You can cut backerboard with power tools, but it will be messier, not any faster, and may damage your blade or motor.

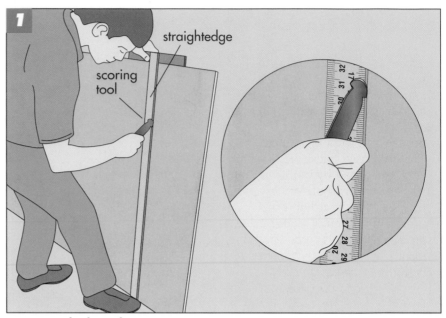

YOU'LL NEED

SKILLS: Measuring, cutting.
TIME: Each cut requires no more than 5–10 minutes.
TOOLS: Drywall square or a straightedge, utility knife or scoring tool, rubbing stone.

1. Score the board.
For cement-based board, measure carefully and mark cut-off lines on both sides of the backerboard. Align a straightedge with the line on one side. Pull the scoring tool along the straightedge; make as many passes as are necessary to break through the mesh on the surface. Place the straightedge on the other side and repeat the process. The mesh must be completely severed on each side. (A faster but somewhat riskier method: Proceed as you would for drywall, cutting one side, snapping the cut edge over, then cutting the other side.)

2. Snap.
Place the backerboard on a flat surface. Press down with your hand on one side of the cut line. With the other hand, lift up just enough to snap the board along the scored edges. Some types of backerboard may break more easily if you elevate the board on one side of the scoring line, then press down.

3. Smooth edges.
Be careful when handling the cut board. Some types of backerboard may leave a sharp edge along the cut line. The best way to smooth the edge is to use a rubbing stone.

TOOLS TO USE

A HOLE SAW

Cement-based backerboard is often used under tiled surfaces in wet areas. That means you may have to fit it over plumbing protrusions in the wall, countertop, or floor. Most holes can be drilled quickly and effectively using a power drill equipped with a carbide-tipped hole saw. The hole saw should be available where you buy your tile or at any large home center. Another method is to mark and score a circle on both sides of the board, then tap through with a hammer.

INSTALLING BACKERBOARD

If it has been cut correctly, backerboard is fairly easy to install. Each type is installed with screws or nails, then the seams are joined with fiberglass tape and mortar. If you are planning to tile in a wet area, remember to take proper waterproofing steps. Cement-based backerboard itself is not damaged by moisture, but it is not waterproof. Water can permeate the board and the underlying framing, causing serious damage. For best results, install a waterproofing membrane behind the backerboard (page 26). Use the type of fasteners recommended by the manufacturer. Roofing nails work, but corrosion-resistant screws offer superior holding power. Edges of backerboard must by supported by studs or joists, or glued with construction adhesive to a sound wall surface.

Attach to walls.
Attach backerboard directly to bare studs or over an existing layer of drywall. In either case, make sure the drywall screws or nails are long enough to penetrate the framing at least ¾ inch.

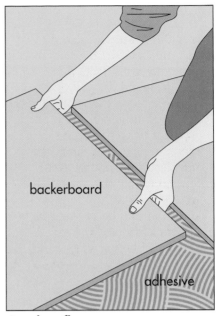

Attach to floors.
Coat the clean subfloor with adhesive applied with a notched trowel. Set the boards so that all joints fall over floor joists. Press the board into the adhesive before fastening with screws.

EXPERTS' INSIGHT

EXPANSION GAPS BETWEEN BOARDS

One of the most important steps you can take to ensure a long-lasting tile installation is to plan for some movement on and below the finished surface. Expansion gaps, filled with a flexible material, allow for normal movement without jeopardizing the integrity of the tile and grout. Each manufacturer has specific recommendations for expansion gaps around board edges. As a general rule, you should leave a ⅛-inch gap between boards and a ¼-inch gap around bathtubs and shower pans.

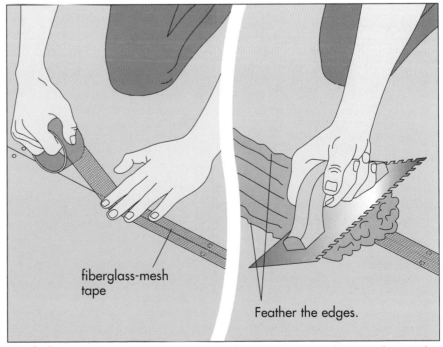

fiberglass-mesh tape

Feather the edges.

Finish the joints.
With all boards fastened, apply adhesive-backed fiberglass-mesh tape to the joints. Holding a trowel nearly flat, spread adhesive over

the tape, pressing it into the mesh. Feather the edges of the adhesive for a smooth finish. Make sure there are no high spots; shallow low spots are not a problem.

MIXING THIN-SET MORTAR

With the setting bed in place, cleaned, and marked for the layout, it is time to prepare the adhesive. For tiling walls, you will probably use an adhesive that does not have to be mixed. For tiling floors, you can use a premixed mortar or floor tile adhesive, but the thin-set mortar that you mix yourself will be the strongest (see page 23).

Mixing will be easier if all the ingredients are at room temperature; buy the powder and any additives in advance and store them overnight in the house. Mixing can get sloppy, especially if you are using a power mixer. Place the bucket in the middle of the area to be tiled, or on top of a dropcloth.

Use a heavy-duty, ½-inch drill for power mixing, as a smaller drill may burn out. Keep a second bucket on hand, about half full of water, for cleaning your mixer.

Mixing by hand.
Mix small batches of thin-set mortar (less than 2 gallons) by hand. Use a trowel or a stiff piece of wood, and make sure you scrape the bottom of the bucket as you stir.

Using a mortar mixer.
Mix larger batches with a mortar mixer mounted on a powerful drill. Clamp the bucket with your feet to keep it from spinning. Set the mixer in, and start mixing with short bursts of power, to keep the mixture from spilling.

EXPERTS' INSIGHT

HOW MUCH TO MIX?
Like other cement-based adhesives, thin-set mortar begins to cure almost as quickly as it is mixed. If you mix too much at once, it may be unusable when you reach the bottom of the bucket. On the other hand, it is a waste of time to mix batches that are too small. Professional tile setters mix enough adhesive to last them somewhere between 30 and 60 minutes. However, if you are working in a room with dry air, you may need to mix less. Experiment with progressively larger batches.

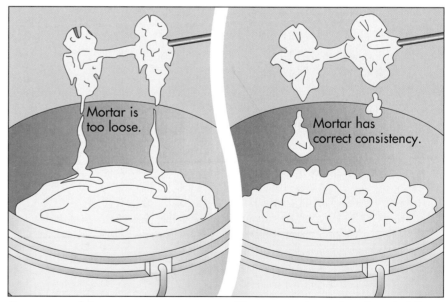

Proper consistency.
It takes some practice and experience to know when the mortar has just the right amount of ingredients. The mix is too loose if it runs off the mixing tool. Add more dry ingredients and mix some more. Lift the mixer again.

The mortar is ready when it falls off, but no longer runs off, the mixing tool. If the mortar starts drying out before you've used it up, discard the batch and mix a new one. Adding more liquid at that point will keep the mortar from adhering well.

SPREADING THIN-SET MORTAR

After mixing the mortar, let it rest for 10 minutes before applying. Scoop a small amount onto the setting surface and comb it with a notched trowel. If the ridges hold their shape and do not flatten out, the batch is ready to spread. Begin spreading mortar at the intersection of your reference lines. Take care not to cover up the lines. Work in small areas. If you've never tiled before, spread only enough to cover 2 or 3 square feet. As you gain experience, you can expand the size of the working area. Packages of thin-set mortar refer to the *open time*—the amount of time you have to set tiles on combed adhesive. Use a margin trowel (see page 21) to scoop adhesive onto the bottom of your notched trowel, or drop dollops of mortar onto the floor and then spread them out. Give the thin-set mortar a quick stir from time to time.

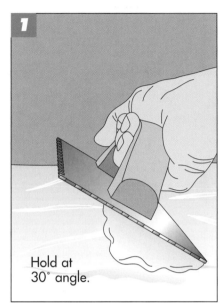

Hold at 30° angle.

1. Apply the thin-set mortar.
Hold the smooth edge of the trowel at a 30-degree angle to the surface. Press adhesive firmly onto the surface. Use sweeping strokes to spread to a consistent depth. Don't cover reference lines.

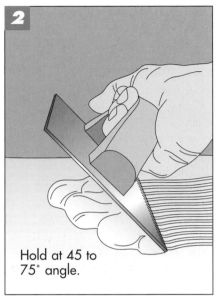

Hold at 45 to 75° angle.

2. Comb the thin-set mortar.
Turn the trowel to the notched edge. Hold the trowel at a 45- to 75-degree angle to form the proper depth of ridge. Comb over the entire surface to produce equally sized ridges.

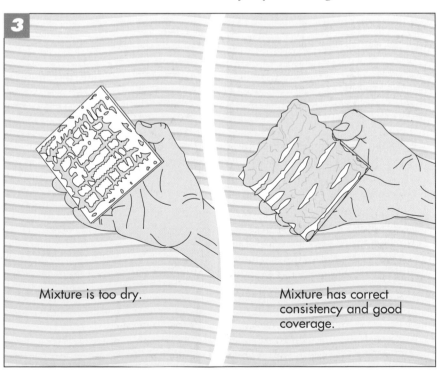

Mixture is too dry.

Mixture has correct consistency and good coverage.

3. Check the coverage.
After spreading and combing a small amount of the mortar, press a tile in place. Twist it a bit so that it is set in the adhesive, then pry it up and look at the bottom. About 75 percent of the surface should be covered. If too little adhesive has stuck to the tile bottom, the mixture is probably too dry.

CAUTION!
WORKING WITH EPOXY ADHESIVE

Epoxy-based adhesives are expensive and tricky to use. Fortunately, they are usually not needed for residential tile jobs. But if you have a setting bed that is incompatible with other adhesives, or are installing tile in an area likely to receive extreme heat, epoxies may be necessary. Read all instructions carefully. Wear a charcoal-filter mask, work in a well-ventilated area, and avoid skin contact with the mixed solution. Mix epoxy adhesive by hand and carefully follow the manufacturer's instructions about the proportion of wet and dry ingredients.

CUTTING TILE

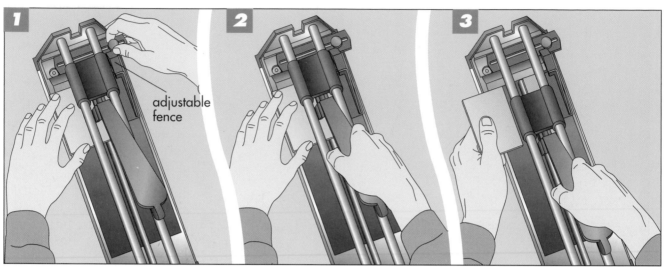

1. To use a snap cutter, mark and position the tile.

Mark a cut line on the tile with a pencil or felt-tipped pen (on glazed tiles only). Place a tile in the cutter, right side up, aligning the cut line with the cutting wheel. Set and lock the fence on the cutter to hold the tile in place.

2. Score the tile.

Hold the tile in place with one hand and the handle with the other. Set the cutting wheel on the top of the tile. Pull or push (depending on your model) the handle while maintaining steady pressure on the tile. Try to score the tile evenly on the first pass.

3. Snap the tile.

When the tile has been scored, press back on the handle just enough to snap the tile along the score line. If the tile will not break, the score line was probably incomplete or not deep enough.

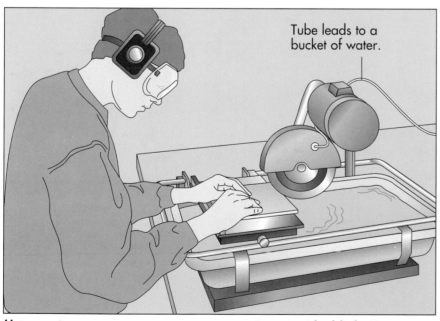

Tube leads to a bucket of water.

Use a wet saw.

Wear safety glasses and hearing protection. See that the blade is in good condition, and that the water bucket is full. Place the tile on the sliding table, and lock the fence to hold the tile in place. Turn the saw on, and make sure water is running onto the blade. Press down on the tile as you slide it through, taking care to keep your fingers out of the way. When the water runs out, refill the bucket; do not cut with the saw for even a few seconds unless water is running onto the blade.

CAUTION!

BEWARE OF EDGES

One of the advantages of a wet saw is that it makes very smooth cuts. You can create razor-sharp edges when using a snap cutter or tile nippers. After cutting the tile, immediately smooth those edges. Grasp the tile on an uncut edge. Move a rubbing stone back and forth over the cut side, smoothing and rounding over the edge as you go. If you do not have a rubbing stone, you can achieve the same result with carbide-grit sandpaper. Use a sanding block, or wrap the sandpaper around a block of wood.

TRIMMING TILE

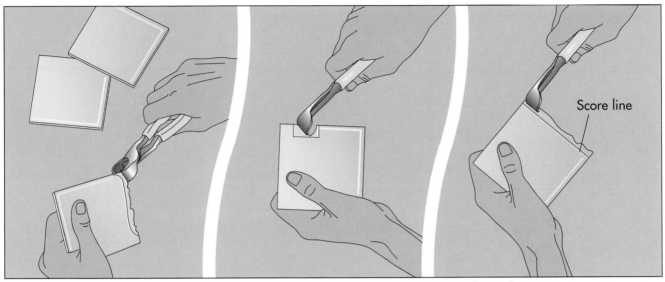

Score line

Use tile nippers for a curved cut...

For cuts that are not straight, use a rod saw (see below), or tile nippers. (Most floor tiles cannot be cut with a rod saw, so you will need to use nippers.) Practice on scrap pieces of tile to get the hang of it. Hold the nippers roughly parallel to the cut line, and bite away small chunks.

for a notch...

If the notch will have square corners, use a snap cutter to score at least some of the lines; this will make it a bit easier to nibble precisely up to the lines. Nibbling a notch requires patience. Bite away only a little at a time, or you may break the whole piece.

or for a sliver.

Nippers are also useful for very narrow straight cuts when you do not have a wet saw. Use the snap cutter or a glass cutter to score the glaze on the tile. Place the jaws close to, and parallel with, the score line. Take a series of bites along the cut line.

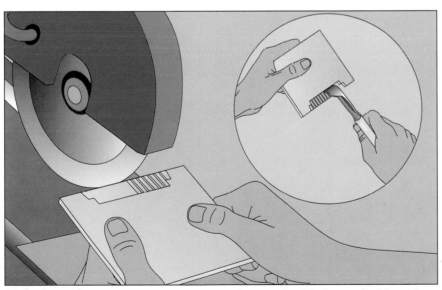

Make irregular cuts.

Use a wet saw to make irregular cuts that would take a long time to accomplish with nippers. To make a series of closely spaced, parallel cuts with the wet saw, hold the tile in your hands. Rest your hands on the sliding table as you move the

tile into the blade. By holding the tile at the correct angle, you can produce a series of cuts that all end at the cut line. Break off the tile pieces with your fingers or nippers, then clean up the cut edge with a rubbing stone.

TOOLS TO USE

THE ROD SAW

A rod saw is a cylindrical hacksaw blade made of tungsten carbide. If you are on a tight budget or do not have very many odd-shaped cuts to make, this tool can be a handy accessory. Set the rod saw snugly in the hacksaw body, firmly support the tile, and cut using a sawing motion. With a rod saw you can cut fairly quickly through wall tiles, but it will be rough going—and perhaps impossible—with floor tiles. A rod saw is useful for cutting tight curves.

SETTING TILE

When the adhesive has been combed to the right thickness, immediately begin setting tiles. The most important tile is the first one you set; make sure that it is aligned perfectly with your layout so that the rest of the tiles will fall into place nicely. You will be rewarded at this stage for having spent all that time on the layout. Your reference lines will help to guide you through the entire process; take care not to cover them over with adhesive.

Work in sections small enough to set the tiles before the adhesive begins to dry out. Start by spreading adhesive in a 2- to 3-square-foot area; set the tiles and remove excess adhesive before moving on to the next section. With practice, you can work in larger sections. If the adhesive has begun to skin over, do not set tiles in it. Rather, scoop up and discard the adhesive and apply a fresh layer.

Whenever possible, set all full tiles first, then set the cut tiles. But also avoid kneeling on top of just-set tiles in order to lay the cut ones. On a large job, you might want to set all of the full tiles one day, then handle the cut tiles the next day.

Take care not to tile yourself into a corner. Set tiles so that you can leave the room without walking on them. Don't disturb floor tiles until the adhesive has cured—preferably overnight.

YOU'LL NEED

TIME: About one hour for every 3 to 5 square feet of field tiles; small, complex installations take two to three times as long.
SKILLS: Setting tiles into the adhesive; cutting tiles to fit.
TOOLS: Beating block and hammer, putty knife or trowel, sponge, tile cutter.

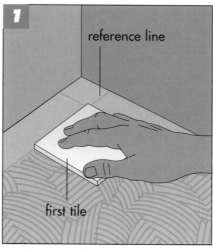

reference line

first tile

1. Begin at the corner.

With the adhesive spread, place the first tile at the intersection of the reference lines. Press and twist it slightly into place, aligning the tile with both lines. Do not slide the tile through the adhesive.

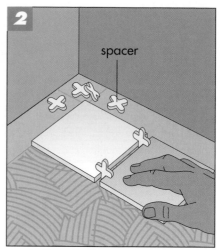

spacer

2. Follow the layout.

Place another tile next to the first. Use spacers unless the tiles are self-spacing. Press and twist the tile to ensure that it is fully embedded in the adhesive. Accurate placement of the first few tiles is critical.

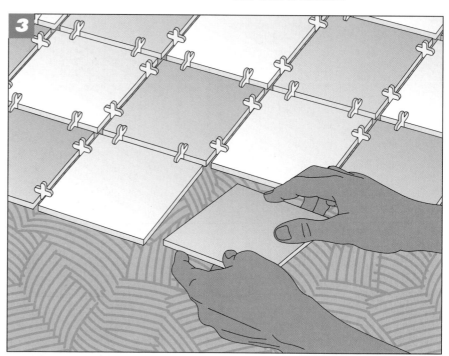

3. Fill in the field.

Continue setting tiles along the layout lines in the section. Then set the tiles in the field, working out from the corner. Insert spacers as shown. (Spacers can also be laid flat at the intersection of the grout lines, but must be removed before grouting.) If the tiles are self-spacing, keep an eye on the gaps between tiles to make sure that they remain uniform. Avoid sliding the tiles once they have been set in the adhesive. Check the backs of the tiles from time to time to see that they are adhering properly.

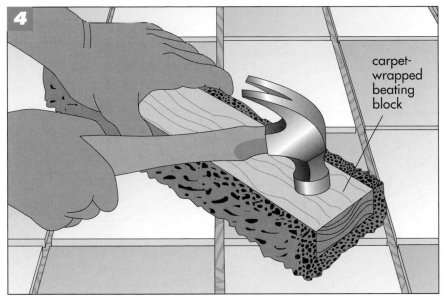

carpet-wrapped beating block

4. Use a beating block.

After setting tiles in one section, use a beating block (see page 20 for tips on making a beating block) to ensure a level surface and full adhesion. Place the beating block so that it spans several tiles, and give it a few light taps with a hammer. Make sure each tile gets tapped this way.

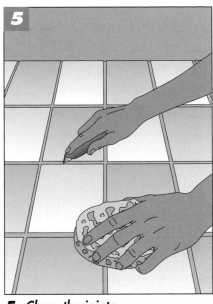

5. Clean the joints.

Immediately after setting tiles in each section, go back and remove excess adhesive before it starts to dry. Clean the tile surfaces with a damp sponge, and use a putty knife or margin trowel to remove excess from between tiles.

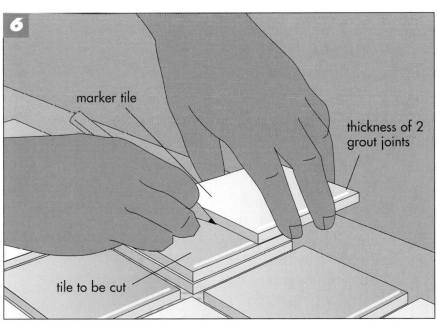

marker tile

thickness of 2 grout joints

tile to be cut

6. Cut tiles last.

When all of the full tiles have been set in the field, begin setting cut tiles around the perimeter. Since walls are rarely square, it is usually best to cut one tile at a time. The safest method is to measure each tile "in place." Set the tile to be cut directly on top of the adjacent tile. Then set another full tile on top, two grout joints away from the wall. Use the top tile to mark the cut line.

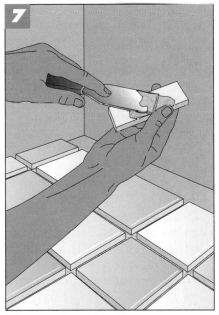

7. Back-buttering tiles.

When you are unable to use a trowel to apply the adhesive on the setting surface, *back-butter* individual tiles: Use a notched trowel or a putty knife, depending on the size of the tile, and spread adhesive on the back. Use enough adhesive so that the tile will be level with other tiles.

SETTING MOSAIC TILE

Historically, tile mosaic has been an elaborate decorative technique using small pieces of tile, stone, and shells set one by one to produce unique patterns. Today, mosaic tiles are almost always sold in sheets, with small tiles held together by a mesh or paper backing, or with small adhesive dots. These sheets make installation much quicker than setting tiles individually. You can find mosaic tiles in a variety of patterns, glazed and unglazed. Glass mosaic tiles are available in 1-inch squares. Mosaic tiles are particularly suitable for use on floors, but are also popular for walls and countertops.

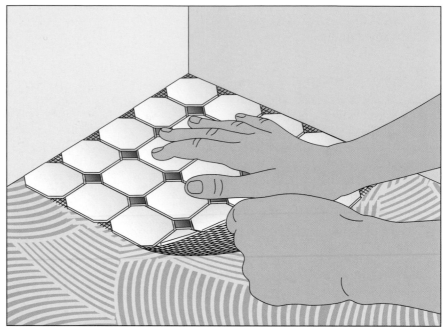

Set mosaic tiles.
Back-mounted mosaic tiles should be set in thin-set mortar. Because various backing materials perform differently, check with the supplier for any special instructions. Take care to ensure that each individual tile on a sheet is fully embedded in the adhesive. Move a beating block slowly across the whole sheet, lightly tapping it as you go.

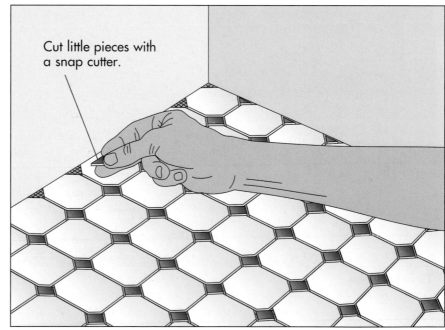

Cut little pieces with a snap cutter.

Cut mosaics.
One advantage of small mosaic tiles is that you can often manage an installation without having to cut individual tiles. Use a utility knife to cut strips of tiles away from the sheet. If you do need to fill in spaces with small, cut tiles, remove the tiles from the backing and cut them with a snap cutter or nippers. Back-butter the tiles with adhesive before setting.

EXPERTS' INSIGHT

ARRANGING PATTERNS
Sheets of mosaic tiles are sometimes composed of randomly arranged tiles in a variety of colors. This randomness looks best when it has a balance to it; colors should be scattered around the surface, not clumped together. You can control the balance somewhat by planning the arrangement of the tile sheets. Before you start spreading adhesive and setting the tiles, take time to study the patterns on individual sheets. You may find that some sheets look better than others when placed next to each other. Some mosaic sheets are set according to a pattern. In that case, install the tiles so that you continue, rather than disrupt, the pattern.

WORKING WITH IRREGULARLY SHAPED TILE

Handmade paver tiles lend a pleasing informality to a room. Mexican tiles, *saltillos*, are one common choice; they have the added benefit of being very inexpensive. Handmade tiles will not be uniformly shaped; they can vary widely in shape, thickness, size, and color from tile to tile. Choose the tiles by inspecting each one and discarding those with severe blemishes.

Irregularly shaped tiles present several installation challenges. Not only are sizes unpredictable, but some of them may be significantly warped. Tiles of different thicknesses can create a tripping hazard if not installed with care. Since the backs often are not flat, back-butter each tile with adhesive. Handmade tiles cannot be cut easily with a snap cutter; a wet saw is much more effective. Some types require application of a sealer before grouting.

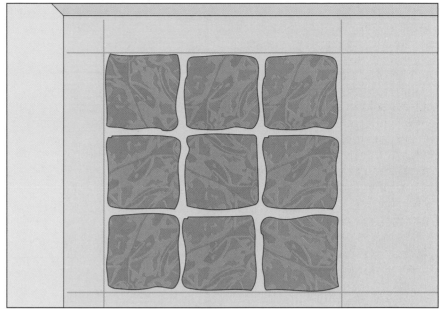

Floor layout for irregular pavers.
When the tiles are not of predictably uniform size, layout becomes less precise. Rather than using plastic spacers, break the layout into a grid. For tiles that are approximately 12 inches square, use chalk lines to make 3-foot squares; each square will hold nine tiles. Dry-fit the tiles first, adjusting the spaces between them by sight. Then set the tiles one square at a time.

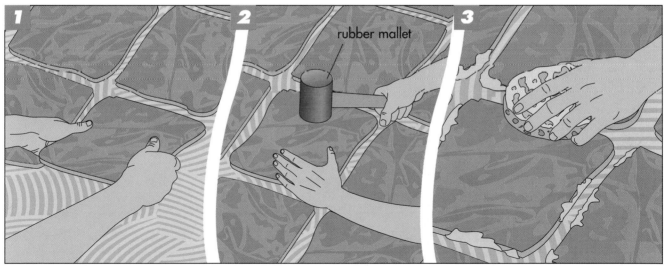

rubber mallet

1. Set the tiles.
Comb on thin-set mortar (page 39). For tiles with irregular backs, apply adhesive on the backs as well to ensure an adequate bond. To make sure you can compensate for warped tiles and varying thicknesses, use a trowel with ½-inch notches to spread the adhesive.

2. Tap with a mallet.
With uniform, machine-made pavers, you can use a beating block as described on page 43. With handmade pavers, however, tap on each tile individually. Use a soft mallet, not a hammer.

3. Clean the tiles.
Remove mortar that oozes up between the tiles. Take care to keep mortar off the surface of the tiles. Before grouting, clean the tiles with a sponge and water. Apply sealer to unsealed tiles before grouting.

WORKING WITH STONE TILE

Stone tiles are made from stone that is quarried all over the world. Many types are available, and they vary widely in color and price. Polished stone has a shiny, almost glazelike finish that looks best on walls and interior floors. Honed stone has a smooth, matte finish that does not show wear as much as does polished stone. If properly sealed, honed tiles can be used in wet areas where polished stone would be too slippery. Flamed stone has a rough finish that is most useful on heavily traveled floors. Most stone is brittle, so the substrate must be strong—at a minimum, backerboard over ¾-inch plywood or a thick mortar bed. Because stone is heavy, be sure your floor joists are strong enough to hold it. Check with an engineer or architect if you are not sure. Cut stone tile with a wet saw, and use a blade suitable for the type of stone you are cutting.

TYPES OF STONE

Type	Description	Pros	Cons
Marble	A limestone that has been changed deep beneath the earth's surface into a hard composition of crystals. Characterized by varied patterns and colors of veins.	Elegant appearance, used in many of the world's most famous buildings; beautiful and long lasting.	Veins add to appeal, but weaken the marble. Dark-colored marble can fade in sunlight. Easily scratched and stained.
Granite	Quartz-based stone with a tough, glossy appearance. Colors range from light to dark, with varying patterns and graining.	Harder than marble; resists scratching. Easy to care for; resists acids. Excellent choice for kitchen countertops. Generally very dense and capable of withstanding freeze-thaw cycles.	Quarried all over the world, with varying characteristics from each region. Softer granites can sometimes show wear.
Slate	A rough-surfaced tile that is split, rather than sliced, from quarried stone. Available in slabs or as cut tiles, usually 12 inches square. Gauged slate is ground smooth on the bottom, while ungauged (or cleft) slate is rough on both sides.	Widely available and reasonably priced.	Somewhat brittle, with less range of colors than other stones. Dark slate may fade in sunlight. Irregular surface can produce undesirable flooring. Ungauged slate needs to be set in a thick mortar bed.

Materials to Use with Stone Tile

Be sure to get the right materials for setting, grouting, and sealing your stone tiles.

■ Latex-modified thin-set mortar works for most installations, but epoxy thin-set may be needed. Do not use organic mastics. Marble is somewhat transparent, so use white thin-set rather than gray.

■ With ceramic tile, a contrasting grout color is often used as part of the design. With stone tile, and especially with marble and granite, the objective is usually to minimize or eliminate the visual impact of the grout joints, so the surface resembles a solid whole. Choose a grout color that closely matches the stone. Use unsanded grout with marble and slate tiles, and epoxy adhesive as grout with closely spaced granite tiles.

■ Clear sealers can improve the appearance of stone tile and protect it from dirt, water, and stains. Use a low-sheen penetrating sealer on a floor; glossy sealers work well with other surfaces. Choose a sealer recommended for your type of stone. Test on a scrap tile to make sure it won't discolor your tiles. Granite usually needs no sealer.

EXPERTS' INSIGHT

SHOPPING FOR STONE

Often the most attractive stones are the weakest because of their deep veins. Stone tiles are often sorted according to their background color, but variations within the sorted colors can be substantial. Look through each box of tiles before you buy. Get extras so you can return tiles that are unsatisfactory. Buy only from a knowledgeable and reputable dealer.

SETTING GRANITE AND MARBLE TILE

Granite and marble are usually quarried and then manufactured to uniform sizes and thicknesses. Standard tiles are 12 inches square and ⅜ inch thick, with one side polished smooth. To minimize chipping, the exposed edges of granite and marble tiles are beveled. In fact, the edges are usually so smooth and straight that the grout joint between tiles can be very thin; sometimes the tiles are installed without any grout joints at all. Do a complete dry run before applying adhesive and laying tiles.

YOU'LL NEED

TIME: About a day for a 12-foot-long countertop.
SKILLS: Cutting and setting tiles, careful alignment of tiles.
TOOLS: Wet saw or grinder with a diamond blade.

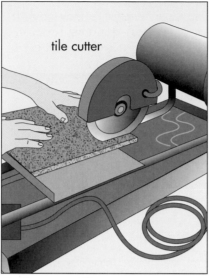

Cutting stone tiles.
Use a wet saw. Natural stone sometimes breaks along existing fissure lines when you try to cut it. If this becomes a problem, cut the tile through only two-thirds of its thickness, then flip it over and finish the cut from the other side.

TOOLS TO USE

STONE CUTTER

The best tool for making neat rectangular cutouts is a small stone cutter equipped with a diamond blade. Rent or borrow one from the tile dealer or a rental store. (Tile setters often mount a diamond blade on an electric grinder.) After cutting in each direction, knock the cutout free, and use tile nippers and a rubbing stone to clean up the corners.

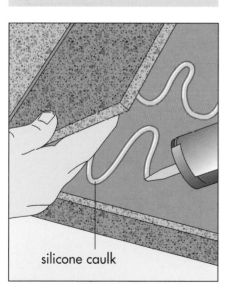

Set in silicone caulk.
It may not look professional, but many tile setters use this technique. After you have done a complete dry run and know exactly where each tile will go, lift up one or two tiles at a time and make squiggles of clear silicone caulk on the substrate. Set the tiles in it quickly but carefully.

Seal it first.
Manufacturers recommend that some types of stone tiles be set with an expensive epoxy mortar. An alternative technique is to coat the back of the tiles with nonporous epoxy. Once the coating has dried, the tiles can be set with regular thin-set mortar.

Finish the edge.
You can buy special edging tiles for some types of stone. Or install narrow strips on the edge, and set the tiles on top of them, to produce the illusion of a massive slab. Have the exposed edges polished by the dealer, or polish them with a rubbing stone, and perhaps brush on several coats of clear lacquer.

GROUTING TILE

Grout is a thin mortar mixture that is used to fill the joints between tiles. It protects tile edges from nicks and cracks, and it helps keep water from working its way below the tile surface. The size and color of the grout joint can be as important to the finished appearance of a floor or wall as the tile itself. So it pays to choose and apply the grout carefully. (See page 25 for more on grout selection.) Do not apply grout until the adhesive has set, which normally takes up to 24 hours. If you are tiling more than one surface, such as a bathroom floor and walls, set the tiles on all the surfaces before you begin grouting. Then grout the walls before the floor. For stronger and less permeable grout, mix the powder with latex additive rather than water.

YOU'LL NEED

TIME: Several hours for a typical bathroom floor.
SKILLS: Mixing and spreading grout, shaping grout joints, careful cleanup.
TOOLS: Bucket, trowel, or mortar mixer; awl; rubber gloves; grout float; sponge; joint shaper.

CAUTION!
USING COLORED GROUT
If you are using colored grout, mix a small test batch. Let it dry so you can see the finished color. Also, spread some of the grout on a scrap tile to see if it stains the tile surface. When adding color additive to grout, mix it in before adding the liquid. And make note of the exact quantities of ingredients used so that you can mix consistent colors from one batch to the next.

1. Mix by hand...
Measure the liquid and pour it into the bucket. Add the dry ingredients a little at a time. Stir cautiously with a clean trowel or piece of wood. Add more dry ingredients as needed.

or use a mortar mixer.
For preparing large amounts, use a mortar mixer attached to an electric drill. Set the blade in the mixture, then mix at a slow speed. Don't lift the blade out until it has stopped turning.

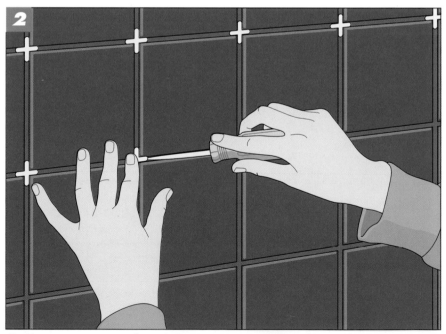

2. Remove spacers, clean joints.
Before you begin spreading grout, remove all of the spacers between tiles. An awl or some other thin tool will make removal easier. Also, remove any adhesive that was squeezed into the joints between tiles. A razor blade or grout saw will speed this process. Vacuum the joints, and put masking tape over all expansion joints, which will be caulked later.

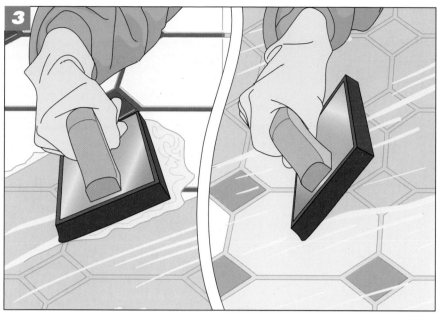

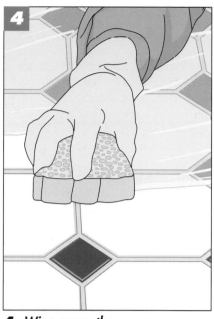

3. Apply the grout.

For a floor, put enough grout on the tiles to cover about 3 square feet. For a wall, scoop up a good-sized dollop with the float. Hold the grout float at about a 35-degree angle, and spread the grout diagonally across the tiles. Press the grout firmly and completely into the joints. Make two or three passes, working in a different direction for each pass.

Tilt the float up so it is nearly perpendicular to the surface, and wipe away excess grout. Move diagonally to the joints, to avoid digging into them with the float.

4. Wipe away the excess.

When you have finished grouting one area, use a dampened sponge to wipe the tiles. Use a circular motion. If the grout is hard to wipe from the tiles, don't wait so long next time. Take care that the joints are consistent in depth. Rinse the sponge often.

TOOLS TO USE

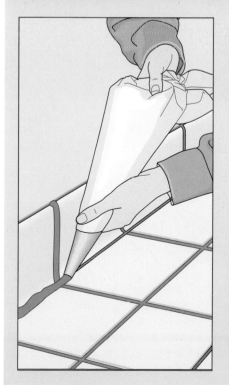

A GROUT BAG

A grout (or mortar) bag looks a bit like a pastry bag used for decorating cakes. It is useful for grouting joints that can't be reached with a trowel, or for particularly porous tiles that soak up grout quicker than you can clean it off the surface. Use a tip on the grout bag no wider than the width of the joint. Fill the bag with grout, then place the tip in the joint. Move the bag as you squeeze grout into the joint. Grout the full length of joints rather than grouting around each tile. Let the grout harden a little, then shape the joints. Once the grout has set for 30 minutes or more, sweep the joints with a broom or stiff brush to remove the excess.

EXPERTS' INSIGHT

ALLOW FOR EXPANSION

Don't forget about the expansion joints. These joints at corners and edges must be filled with expandable caulk, which allows the surfaces to expand and contract without cracking or damaging the tiles. Use masking tape to keep grout out of the expansion joints. Some grout will still seep under the tape and into the joint. So when you have finished grouting, remove the tape and clean out the grout. Or wait for it to dry, and cut it out with a grout saw or utility knife. Let the joint dry completely, and vacuum before caulking.

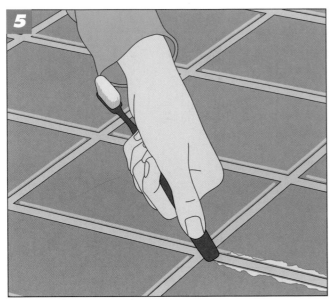

5. Shape the joints.

After wiping the tiles, clean and shape the joints. Pull a barely dampened sponge along grout lines, removing high spots as you go. Some people like thick grout lines that are nearly flush with the surface of the tile, while others prefer grout lines that recede. The important thing is that they be consistent. Buy an adjustable grout shaper, or use a toothbrush handle or a wood dowel. The shaper should be a bit wider than the joint.

6. Fill the gaps.

If you notice a gap or inadvertently pull grout out from a joint, fill it right away with grout. Wearing rubber gloves, press a small amount into the void, filling it completely. Then shape the joint and remove any excess grout.

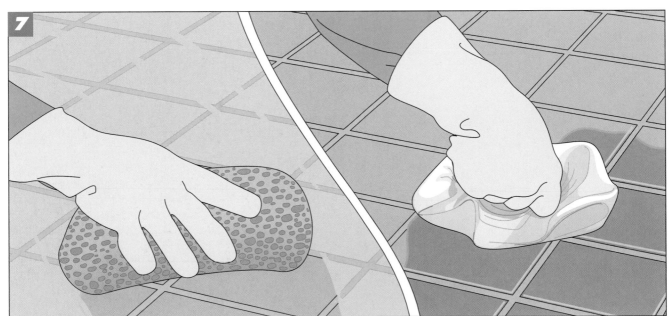

7. Remove the grout film.

Once you have cleaned the tile surfaces of grout and shaped the joints, let the grout set up for another 15 to 20 minutes. With your sponge and a bucket of clean water, and wearing a rubber glove, start the final cleaning of the tiles. Timing is critical: The grout should be dry enough to not be affected by the sponge, yet haze on the tile surface should be not so dry that it is difficult to remove. Rinse the sponge and wring it out. Pass the sponge slowly over a line of tiles. Flip the sponge over and make another straight run. Rinse the sponge and continue. With proper timing and careful execution, this process should remove nearly all of the grout residue from the tile surface. After another 15 minutes, polish the tiles with a dry piece of cheesecloth or a clean rag.

CAULKING AND SEALING

Caulk fills expansion joints around the perimeter of a tiled surface. Its flexibility allows adjacent surfaces to expand and contract without damaging tile; and it won't crack, as grout would. Many fine tile jobs have been marred by ugly caulking, so take the time to do it right. (See page 27 for information on choosing caulk.) Practice on scrap pieces until you feel you've got the knack. Place the tube in the gun, cut the tip, and puncture the seal with a long nail. Some people like to cut the tip at a severe angle, while others like to cut it nearly straight across. Have a damp rag handy, soaked with water or mineral spirits, depending on the type of caulk you are using.

YOU'LL NEED

TIME: Less than an hour for most projects.
SKILLS: Applying and smoothing caulk; using a paint roller.
TOOLS: Caulk gun, paint roller and tray or paint brush, rag.

EXPERTS' INSIGHT

GROUT SEALERS
You can significantly improve the durability of grout joints by sealing them. Wait until the grout has fully cured—a week or two—before applying grout sealer. Use a disposable foam-rubber paint brush, which allows you to cover the grout without getting sealer on the tile. Allow the first coat to dry, then apply a second. Renew the grout sealer from time to time.

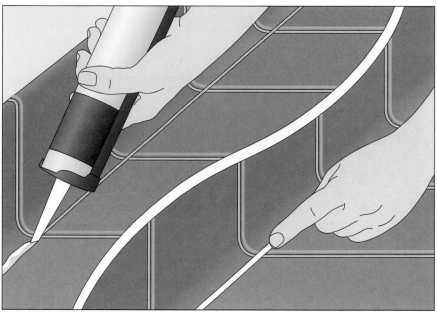

Apply and tool caulk.
Position the tip of the tube on the surface to be caulked, and get yourself into a comfortable position. Squeeze the trigger carefully until caulk begins to flow. Continue squeezing as you pull the gun along. Either leave the bead of caulk as it is, or use a finger or damp rag to smooth it. Strive for a consistent-looking line.

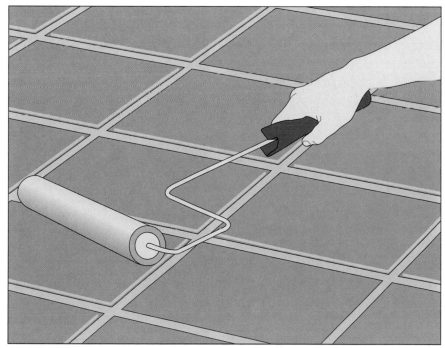

Seal the tile.
Some tiles must be sealed when they are installed, or must have a sealer reapplied every few years. Check with the tile manufacturer for specific instructions. If you are installing unsealed tiles, you may have to apply the sealer before grouting. Otherwise, renew the sealer as needed. A foam-rubber paint roller works well for most types of tile sealer.

DESIGNING A TILE FLOOR

Floor tiles are available in so many sizes, shapes, and colors that the most difficult part of the project often is deciding on a pattern. Not only do you have many choices in tile color and texture, but you can achieve different effects by adjusting the tiles and grout joints. Use one color of tile with matching grout to achieve a unified look often welcomed in small rooms. Or use a contrasting grout to call attention to the individual tiles themselves. Alternate two or more colors of tiles in a pattern or randomly to enliven a room. If you opt for this approach, look for a neutral grout that blends well with your tile colors. Keep the scale of the room and the tile design in harmony: In small spaces, use patterns on a small scale and limit color variety. In larger rooms, feel free to experiment with bolder contrasts.

ABOVE: *Often it's best to let the material itself set the tone. In this bathroom, luxurious marble tiles form a handsome setting for a rug that imitates mosaic tile. Running the tile up the tub surround and wall gives a clean unity to the room. Accent colors can change over the years with this design choice; a beautiful groundwork is in place.*

LEFT: *The graceful sweep of this tiled entryway perfectly suits the contemporary style of this home, while providing hardworking utility where it is needed. The pattern of the tiles is straightforward; it's the shape of the platform that sets this floor apart. If your project calls for revising your floor structure, plan ahead to take the final configuration of the tiled surface into consideration. Often it is best after purchasing tile to do a dry run to determine the best possible pattern, and then frame the floor.*

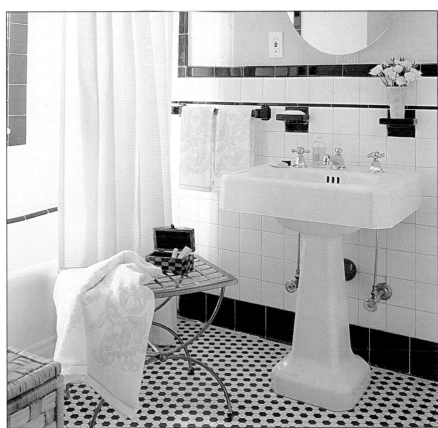

ABOVE: With French doors opening directly onto the backyard, the wearability of tile makes a lot of sense for this bay. The unusual offset of this herringbone pattern suits the shape of the space and is suitable for a variety of decorating styles. Set at a slight angle to the outermost bay, there is an informality to the layout that contrasts pleasantly with the formality of the furnishings.

RIGHT: A bathroom classic, sheet-laid hexagonal tiles in basic black and white will serve for decades and be a backdrop for whatever accent colors you choose to use in the room. Another benefit of this tile design is its structural flexibility. Should the substrate deteriorate with the years, cracks will tend to follow the grout line rather than run through the tiles themselves.

TILING FLOORS

Floors generally are built strong enough to readily accommodate the installation of carpeting or resilient flooring. But ceramic tile has much more demanding requirements. The weight of the tiles is not usually the problem; deflection is. If a ceramic tile floor flexes, grout and even tiles can crack. If you have any doubts about the strength of the floor, ask a contractor to inspect it before you begin tiling.

Sometimes a bouncy floor can be firmed up by driving screws through the subflooring and into joists. Or, you may have to add another subfloor layer, or even beef up the joists. However, if you build up the floor so much that the new tile surface will be a half inch or more higher than an adjacent floor surface, it will look and feel awkward.

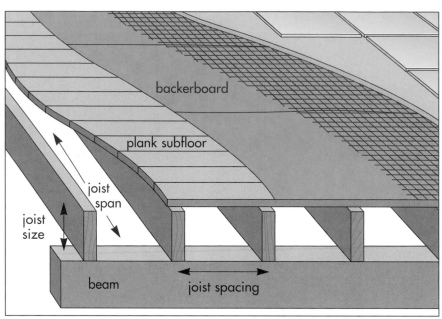

Anatomy of a floor.
Floor joist strength is determined by the size of the joist, the length of the joist's span between supports, and the amount of space between joists. If your joists have spaces larger than 16 inches between them, for instance, then you will need an extra strong subfloor. If you are not sure whether your floor is strong enough, consult with a professional. Plywood is the best subfloor material, but many older homes have strong subfloors made of 1× lumber.

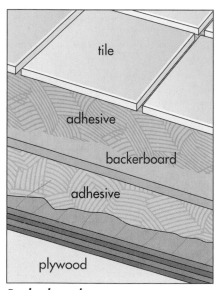

Backerboard
Older installations set tiles on a thick bed of mortar. Backerboard is an excellent modern-day substitute. Use as thick a board as possible installed over a plywood subfloor. See pages 36-37 for cutting and installation instructions.

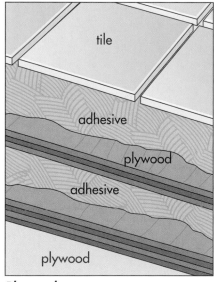

Plywood
Although plywood is somewhat soft and flexible, it also has great strength. And when two sheets are laminated together, the result is a very firm surface.

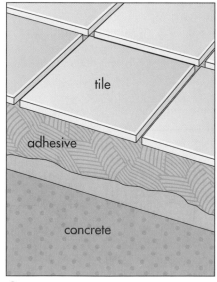

Concrete
Concrete is the best subsurface, and works well for straightening out-of-level floors. Do not use curing or acceleration chemicals if you pour a concrete floor. An older concrete surface must be sound; tiling will not strengthen it.

Preparing a wood floor.

If you will be tiling directly over plywood, it is best to install two layers of ⅝-inch-minimum plywood, rather than one thick sheet. Use exterior-grade A/C (one good side) plywood for the top layer. The edges should always fall over a joist, but stagger the sheets so that the joints do not fall directly over each other. Coat the bottom sheet with construction adhesive before setting the top sheet in place. Leave a gap of ⅛ inch or more around all edges of the top sheets, including at the joints. Fasten the plywood with screws or ring-shank nails. If an existing plywood subfloor is strong enough, remove any high points with a large razor-type scraper made for this purpose. Sand the surface thoroughly, then vacuum. Talk to your tile dealer about the best adhesive to use.

If the existing floor is composed of 1× or 2× planking in good condition, drive screws into joists wherever it seems at all loose, and perhaps install a layer of plywood over it. If it has cracks and does not feel strong, remove the planking and install plywood.

Preparing a concrete floor for tile.

Concrete is a great base for tile, as long as it is structurally sound and flat. Some slabs may actually be too smooth, and should be roughened a bit by grinding with an abrasive wheel. Do not install tile over concrete that was treated with a curing or acceleration chemical when it was poured. These additives will prevent adhesive from bonding properly. If you are uncertain about whether or not such additives were used, try to locate the builder of the house or concrete contractor. They may have a record. You can also test the slab yourself by sprinkling water on it. If the water isn't absorbed, the concrete was probably treated. Apply a latex bonding agent or add a subfloor.

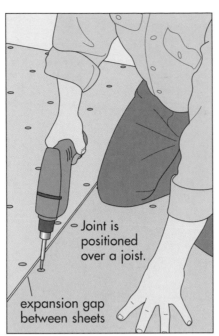

Install plywood.

For the top layer of plywood, leave ⅛-inch gaps between the sheets. Fasten with adhesive and screws or ring-shank nails in a 6-inch grid; every 4 inches at the joints and around the perimeter.

Fill in low spots.

Clean out low spots in a concrete slab and fill with thin-set mortar. Use a trowel or straightedge to level the surface.

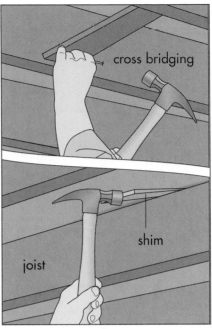

Beef up a wood floor.

Strengthen a weak subfloor by installing wood or metal cross bridging between joists. Close small gaps between joists and the existing subfloor with shims, or drive screws from above.

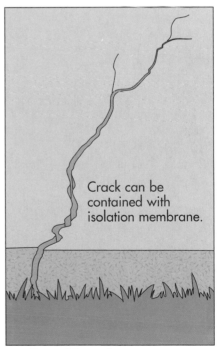

Dealing with cracks.

Cover small cracks in concrete with an isolation membrane (see page 26). Cracks that result in uneven surfaces indicate underlying structural problems; do not tile over such a surface.

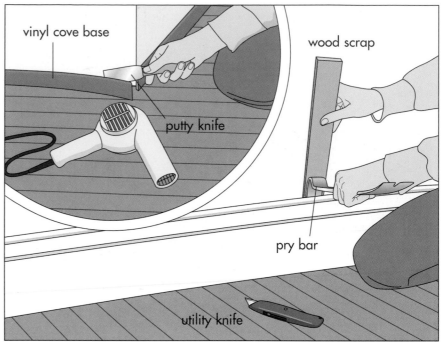

EXPERTS' INSIGHT

REPLACING BASEBOARD

■ As long as you're tiling your floor, you may want to update your baseboards as well. New tile may well emphasize your old baseboard's imperfections.

■ Old vinyl cove base can get rather ratty-looking. Install new cove base after the tile job is done. Make sure that the new material is as wide as the original stuff, or you will have an ugly line on the wall. Apply with cove base adhesive or latex silicone caulk.

■ The shoe (the small, rounded molding at the bottom) gets banged up in time, too. So go ahead and replace it, as well. Use stain or paint on it, then cut it with a miter box and fasten it with finish nails.

Remove the baseboard.

Before tiling a floor, remove the baseboard from the surrounding walls. If the joint between the baseboard and wall is sealed with paint, score it with a utility knife first. Pull vinyl cove base away with a putty knife. If it resists removal, try heating the vinyl with a hair dryer to loosen the adhesive. Use a pry bar to remove wood baseboard. Protect the wall with a thin strip of wood. If your baseboard has a *shoe*—a small rounded molding at the bottom— remove only that molding.

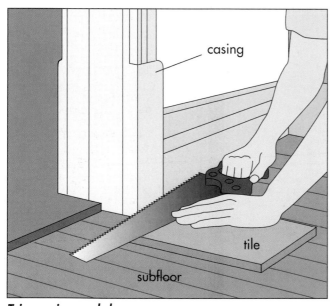

Trim casing and doors.

It is usually not a good idea to remove door casings. But cutting tile to fit around casing is difficult, and usually leads to a sloppy-looking job. So trim the bottom of the casing, and fit the tiles beneath it. With the subfloor installed, place a tile against the casing. Lay a handsaw on the tile to mark the height and keep the saw steady as you cut through the casing.

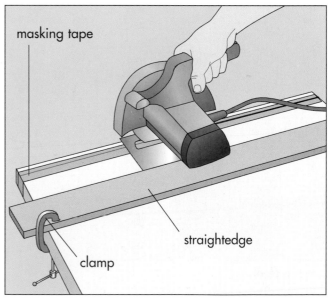

Place tiles on the floor near a door, to make sure it will swing freely after the tiles are installed. If not, use the tiles and a pencil to scribe a cut line at the door's bottom. Allow for a gap of at least ¼ inch. Remove the door by popping out the hinge pins. Place masking tape along the bottom of the most visible side of the door, and mark a cut line. Cut through the tape using a circular saw with a clamped straightedge as a guide.

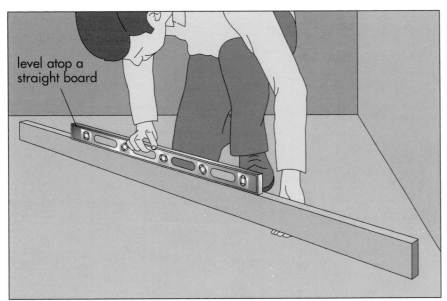

Check floors for level.

Use a carpenter's level and a straight board to check the floor for level and to find any spots that are not flat. If the entire floor is out of level with the wall, it can still be tiled. If you plan to extend tile up the wall, however, you should consider leveling the floor or using tapered baseboard to make the transition attractive.

level atop a straight board

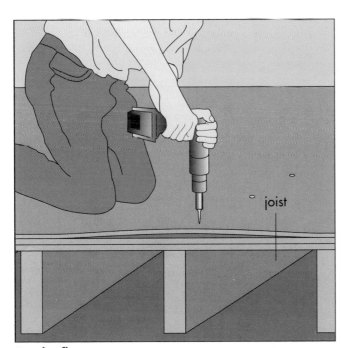

joist

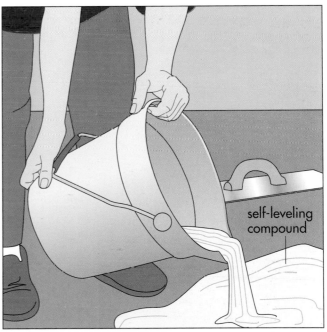

self-leveling compound

Level a floor.

Small bumps in the floor must be dealt with before you begin tiling. If the wood subfloor comes up in places, try driving screws through the flooring and into a joist to level it out. You may be able to take out small high spots with a belt sander.

To straighten out dips and low areas, or to level out an entire floor, use a self-leveling floor patch. These are made by manufacturers of tile adhesive. Place barriers where necessary to keep the compound where it belongs. Mix the dry ingredients with water, then pour it on the floor. The mixture will level itself out to a certain degree, but use a long flat trowel to help things along. The compound should be cured and ready for tiling within a few hours. Most self-leveling compounds are intended to function at depths no greater than 1 inch. If the work seems intimidating, talk to a contractor about preparing a level subfloor for you.

TILING A KITCHEN FLOOR

Tiling a kitchen floor can be a major disruption to any household. This project affects access to food, the preparation of meals, and traffic patterns through the kitchen. Some preparation can be done well in advance of the tiling; some cabinets can be removed, new subflooring applied, and doors removed. For the tiling itself, set aside a long weekend so that the kitchen can be back in operation as quickly as possible.

YOU'LL NEED

TIME: 3–4 days to prepare, lay out, and tile an average-size kitchen.
SKILLS: Disconnecting and removing appliances, removing base cabinets, preparing a subfloor, tiling the floor.
TOOLS: Screwdriver, hammer, pry bar, putty knife.

TOOLS TO USE

KNEE PADS

Tiling floors is hard on your knees. In addition to the stress of kneeling much of the time, your knees are vulnerable to injury from tools and pieces of material left around the work area. That's why contractors who spend a lot of time working at floor level consider knee pads essential. For occasional use on wood or tile floors, nonmarring foam, rubber, or rubber-capped pads are a good choice. (You'll find these useful for gardening as well.) For heavy-duty protection, but less comfort, buy the skateboarder type knee pads that have a hard nylon shield on the front.

1

base cabinet

toekick

1. Assess the cabinets.
As a general rule, there is no need to install tile where it will be covered by cabinet bases or other permanent fixtures. Instead, use a thin pry bar and stiff putty knife to remove the toekick and any molding along the floor. Set tile up to the cabinet. After all the tile is installed and grouted, trim the upper edge of toekick to fit and reinstall it and the molding.

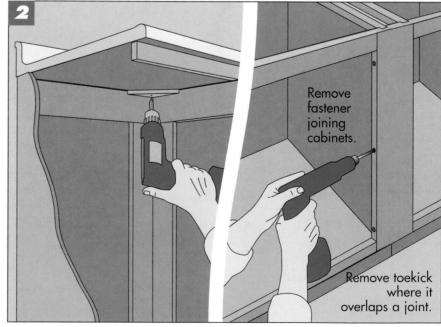

Remove fastener joining cabinets.

Remove toekick where it overlaps a joint.

2. Remove cabinets where needed.
Sometimes cabinets must be removed to take out the old flooring or to replace the subfloor. Remove fasteners holding the countertop in place, and the screws that join cabinets to each other and to the wall. In addition, remove overlapping pieces of toekick and other molding.

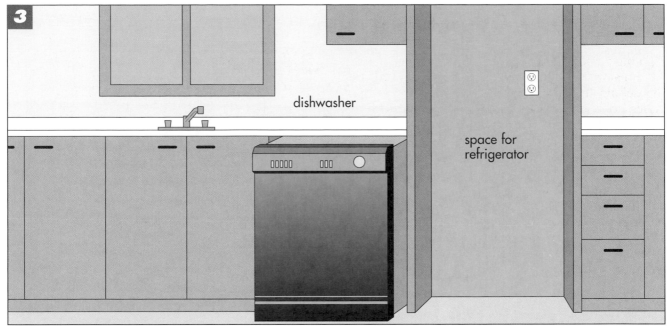

3. Consider the appliances.

One of the issues you will have to address is whether or not to tile beneath appliances. Freestanding appliances, such as refrigerators, ranges, and dishwashers, should be removed from the kitchen to install tile underneath the appliance location. It is also best to tile beneath built-in appliances, although the work can be trickier. Often, by tiling beneath a built-in dishwasher, for example, you raise the floor level such that the dishwasher will no longer fit under the countertop. You can raise or notch out the countertop a bit to accommodate the appliance.

Adjustments may also have to be made to existing plumbing connections. Think of how your kitchen floor would look if it were empty and up for sale. Untiled spaces where appliances usually sit would be unattractive to potential buyers.

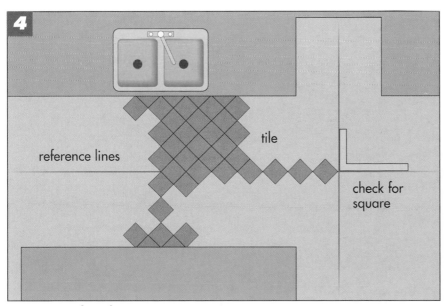

4. Lay out the job.

At the center of the floor, mark perpendicular reference lines with a pencil or chalk line. (In odd-shaped rooms you may want to center the layout on the most visible section of the floor rather than in the center of the room.) Check to make sure that the lines are square (see pages 31–33). Using appropriate spacers, if needed with your tile, dry set tiles along the reference lines to check the layout. Adjust the layout to minimize the number of cut tiles and to avoid creating any extremely small pieces.

5. Set the tiles.

Begin at the intersecting reference lines and spread thin-set mortar over a small area. Do not cover the lines. Set properly spaced tiles. Use a beating block (see page 43) after setting each section of tiles. Check alignment as you go.

TILING A BATHROOM FLOOR

Tile is a great material for bathroom floors: tough, attractive, and easy to clean. Many bathrooms have tile on every surface; plan ahead if you want to resurface your walls, countertops, or tub and shower areas. One of the great joys of tiling a bathroom is the chance to experiment with bold colors and unusual designs.

A typical bathroom floor does not require a waterproof installation, although you should choose tiles and setting materials that are suitable for a surface that will get wet.

YOU'LL NEED

TIME: A full weekend for an average bathroom floor.
SKILLS: Removing and resetting a toilet, preparing a subfloor, laying out and tiling a floor.
TOOLS: Wrench, hacksaw, tiling and grouting tools.

EXPERTS' INSIGHT

REMOVING SINKS

If you have a pedestal or wall-mounted sink with legs, remove it before you start to tile. Shut off the water supply and disconnect the supply lines. Remove the trap with a pipe wrench. Unbolt and remove the top of a pedestal sink, then unbolt and remove the pedestal. (One-piece pedestal sinks are bolted to the floor and wall.) Remove the legs of a wall-mounted sink and pull the sink up and off of the mounting bracket. You may also want to remove a vanity, depending on its position.

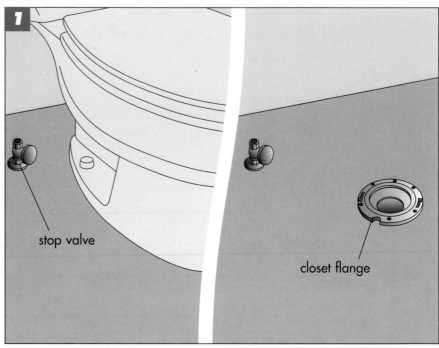

1. Assess the toilet.
When tiling over a finished bathroom floor, the toilet can be left in place. But you will have to cut tiles to fit all around the base, which will probably leave you with an unprofessional-looking job. It is easier in the long run to remove the toilet and tile up to the closet flange. With fewer joints, the tile will look better and pose fewer maintenance problems.

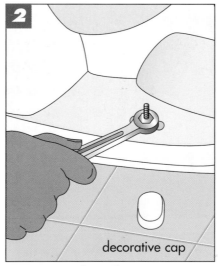

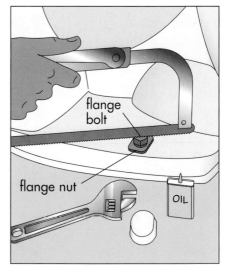

2. Remove the toilet.
Shut off the water supply and disconnect the supply line. Flush the toilet, then sponge the remaining water from the tank. Pry off the decorative caps, then unscrew the flange nuts. If the nut is rusted tight, cut through it with a hacksaw. The easiest way is to cut down, as shown, and then unscrew it. With a helper, lift the toilet off the flange, and carry it to another room. Stuff a rag in the closet flange (make sure it's large enough so it won't fall down the hole) to contain sewer gases, and scrape off any wax, putty, or caulk.

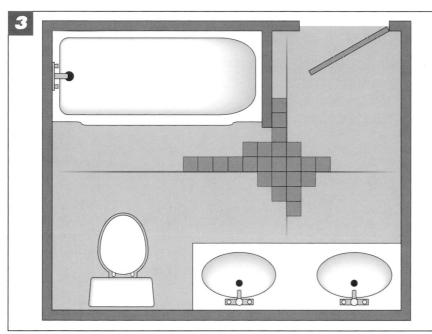

3. Lay out the job.

Small, rectangular bathroom floors are relatively easy to lay out. Arrange grout joints so that they are parallel to the most visible straight edges in the room, such as along counters and tubs. Hide cut tiles in less exposed spots. In such a small area, it is worth your while to check the layout by dry-setting all of the tiles before you begin the installation. See pages 31–33.

4. Set the tiles.

Set full tiles as close as possible to the closet flange. Use nippers to cut tiles to fit around the flange. You don't have to worry about precision here, since the toilet will cover the area.

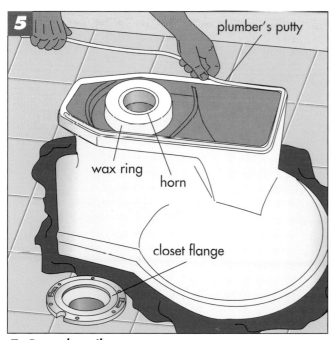

5. Reset the toilet.

After the tile is grouted, reset the toilet. Install new bolts in the flange; they may need to be longer than the old ones. Clean the horn of the bowl and install a new wax ring. If the flange is well below the finished tile surface, add a second wax ring to seal the gap. Run a rope of plumber's putty around the base of the toilet, place it over the bolts. Press down on the toilet to seat it and gently tighten the nuts.

EXPERTS' INSIGHT

TILING OVER TILE

■ When remodeling a bathroom, you may want to replace an old tiled floor with new tiling. Removing the old tile can be a major headache, and it may not be necessary. Instead, you can use the existing floor as a setting bed for the new tile.

■ First, make certain that there are no structural problems with the floor—if the grout is significantly cracked and tiles are loose, it could signal underlying problems that need to be addressed before proceeding. Talk to your tile dealer about the best products and techniques to use over a tiled floor. Normally, the old tiles will need to be sanded heavily, to rough up the glazed surface. You may also need to fill in old grout joints if they aren't level with the tile surface.

■ Keep in mind that the new tile will add to the height of your bathroom floor. Place tiles on top of your existing floor to find out whether this new height will make it awkward to move from the hall into the bathroom. Usually, a threshold will smooth the transition.

TILING AN ENTRYWAY

Most professional tilesetters agree that the best substrate for tile is an old-fashioned mortar bed. But laying it smooth is a job for the pros. Backerboard has made it easier for do-it-yourselfers to install their own tile. There are times, though, when backerboard won't work. This is often the case when you cannot afford to raise the height of the finish floor too much. Entryways frequently pose this dilemma, because the floor connects with several rooms and often a stairway as well. In those situations, a modified mortar-bed installation is best.

YOU'LL NEED

TIME: 2–4 days, depending on the size of the entryway and the amount of preparation needed for the subfloor. Allow time for cement to cure.
SKILLS: Troweling cement to a consistent thickness; preparing a subfloor; tiling a floor.
TOOLS: Steel trowel.

EXPERTS' INSIGHT

BRINGING THE OUTDOORS IN

Often the best types of tile to use for an entryway are those that are commonly used on exterior applications, such as unglazed pavers (machine- or handmade), slate, and half brick. If you also plan to tile an adjacent patio, porch, or other entrance to the house, use matching tiles inside and out to unify the spaces. Be sure the tiles you choose won't become slippery when wet.

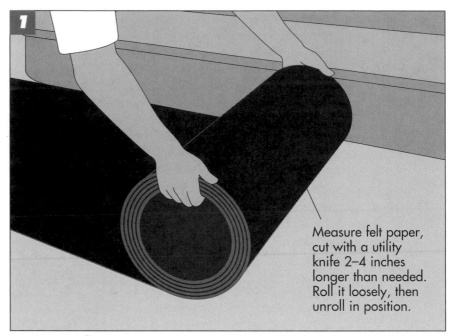

Measure felt paper, cut with a utility knife 2–4 inches longer than needed. Roll it loosely, then unroll in position.

1. Prepare floor.
Stabilize any spongy areas of the floor using drywall screws twice as long as the thickness of your flooring. If necessary, add plywood so your subfloor totals at least 1⅛ inch in thickness. Install 15-pound felt roofing paper overlapping the edges 2 to 3 inches, and staple the paper to the subfloor every 6 to 8 inches. After stapling, trim the edges so the felt doesn't ride up any adjacent molding or stairs.

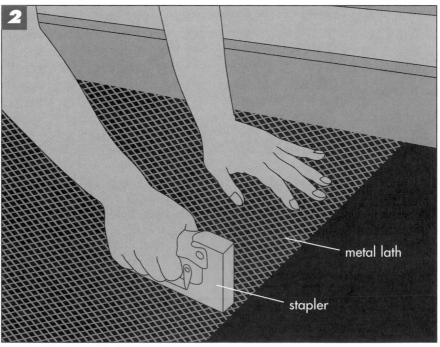

metal lath

stapler

2. Attach metal lath.
Staple galvanized metal lath (mesh) over the felt paper. Available at masonry-supply stores and large home centers in 2-foot-wide strips, the lath can be cut with tin snips. Butt the pieces together; don't overlap them.

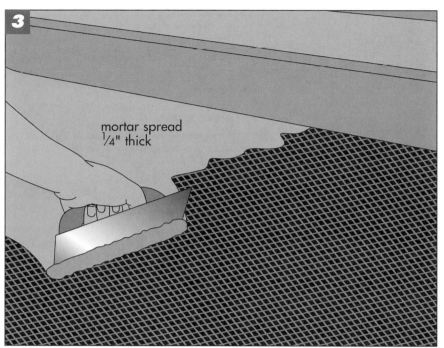

3. Spread the mortar.
Prepare a cement mixture of half portland cement and half fine (builders) sand. The fine sand should not contain stones that would make the surface bumpy. Spread cement with a steel trowel to a depth of ¼ inch, smoothing all ridges. Avoid smearing mortar on stair riser or adjacent molding.

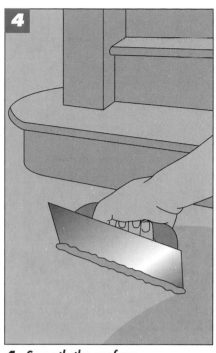

4. Smooth the surface.
Let the mortar cure overnight. Then carefully go over the cement with a trowel to scrape away any high spots. Sweep it to remove any loose material.

5. Lay out and set tiles.
An entryway can be difficult to lay out, because different parts of the floor are visible from different directions. Choose the most public point of view and plan your layout around it. Dry fit the tiles to ensure there won't be any slivers of tile.

6. Grout and seal.
If the tiles were not sealed when you bought them, apply the sealer recommended by the tile maker before grouting. After the tiles are set and grouted (see pages 48–50), wait about a week before applying a liquid topcoat, which should be renewed once or twice a year.

CHOOSING SEALERS AND FINISHES

Grout lines, unglazed tile, and unpolished natural stone are vulnerable to stains, dirt, grease, and mildew. For protection of porous surfaces apply a sealer or finish (the terms are interchangeable). Product types vary according to porosity of the material being covered and the degree of sheen you want. All require that the surface is clean, dry, and free of any other coatings or wax before application. Typically sealers and finishes can be applied in one coat; but for very porous surfaces like brick, two coats are needed. Confirm that the sealer or finish you choose is rated for outdoor use, as some are rated for indoor use only. Use a small paintbrush when sealing the grout alone; apply with a roller when sealing tile and grout.

USING TILE ON WALLS

You can use tile to create a functional, long-lasting, low-maintenance wall covering in any room you like. But what really sets tile apart from other materials and coatings used on walls is the endless creative potential it offers. With floor tiles you are concerned about performance—sustaining heavy loads, holding up to scruffy shoes, not getting too slippery, and ease of cleaning. When choosing wall tiles your focus can shift to color, pattern, texture, and variety. With the exception of large, heavy tiles, virtually any tile available—handmade or factory produced—can be set on a wall. The only limitation is that the substrate be solid enough so there is no flex to crack the grout or tiles.

RIGHT: Tile is one of the few materials that can withstand the heat and grime around a stove while being delightfully decorative.

ABOVE: Beautifully detailed field and border tiles like the ones used in this ornate backsplash can often be found at specialty tile stores or larger home centers. However, if the tile you want is not in stock, check manufacturers' catalogs at your local retailer, or contact tile manufacturers directly for literature. More difficult to find, handmade tiles are more likely to be sold at stores that feature locally produced crafts. An Internet search will turn up a range of potential sources.

ABOVE: By framing an angled field of wall tiles with border tiles, you can install an attractive and easy-to-maintain surface behind your stove and sink areas. Setting the tiles on point breaks the monotony of a tiled wall and sets the wall treatment apart from that used on the countertops. Neutral colors keep the effect subtle.

RIGHT: Tile showrooms often carry a variety of decorative tiles like these border tiles. Local artisans can also be a great source for unique designs. Such specialty tiles as the ones surrounding this bathtub can be expensive. Fortunately, you only need a few of them to create a noticeable effect. In reality, anyone can decorate a tile. Plain or off-white glazed ceramic tiles, paintbrushes, and some water-based ceramic paints are all you need to get started. Create patterns with stencils, or apply paint by dabbing sponges on the tile.

TILING WALLS

Walls often are not very flat. Flexible drywall can be installed over bowed and twisted studs; once it is covered with paint or wallpaper, most people will never notice. But if you try to install tile on an irregular wall, the underlying problem will be magnified. It is very difficult to correct carpentry errors with tile. So check the walls carefully and make necessary corrections before you begin tiling.

YOU'LL NEED

TIME: About one hour per 5 square feet to set and grout tile, plus time for wall preparation.
SKILLS: Checking walls for straightness and squareness, preparing a substrate, installing tile, and grouting.
TOOLS: Level, straightedge, tiling and grouting tools.

1. Assess the walls.
Use a carpenter's level to check walls for plumb. Set a long level or straightedge against the wall at various points to determine if the wall is flat. An out-of-plumb wall can be tiled, but it may affect the appearance of adjoining surfaces. If the wall is not reasonably flat, repair it first.

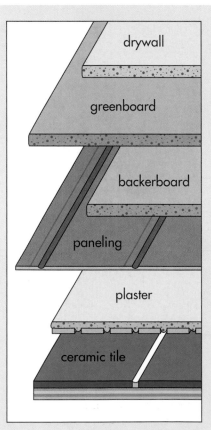

drywall

greenboard

backerboard

paneling

plaster

ceramic tile

WALL SUBSTRATES

Tile can be installed over most existing wall surfaces as long as the wall is flat and in sound condition.

Drywall. The most common wall surface, and a good substrate for tile in dry locations. Can also be used in moderately wet areas if you brush on liquid waterproofing before tiling. Repair holes or cracks with patching compound. Remove wallpaper and loose paint. Lightly sand painted surfaces. Perhaps add a second layer of drywall for added strength or to cover damaged areas.

Moisture-resistant drywall. Commonly known as greenboard or blueboard, it is similar to standard drywall, but is water-resistant—though not waterproof. It can be used in fairly wet areas, but should receive the same waterproofing installation as regular drywall.

Backerboard. An ideal substrate for tile, especially as part of a waterproof installation on shower walls or bathtub surrounds. When installing backerboard over an existing wall surface, use corrosion-resistant nails or screws that are long enough to penetrate the wall studs.

Wall paneling. Most sheet paneling is too thin and fragile to be used as a substrate for tile. Remove the paneling and cover the wall with backerboard or drywall before tiling.

Plaster. Install tile over plaster only if it is hard, flat, and in good condition. If the plaster crumbles when you poke it with a knife, it is too weak and should be replaced with backerboard or drywall. Repair cracks and indentations.

Ceramic tile. You can tile directly over a previously tiled surface as long as it is in good condition. Remove loose or broken tile and fill the cavity with mortar. Aggressively sand the surface to remove any glaze.

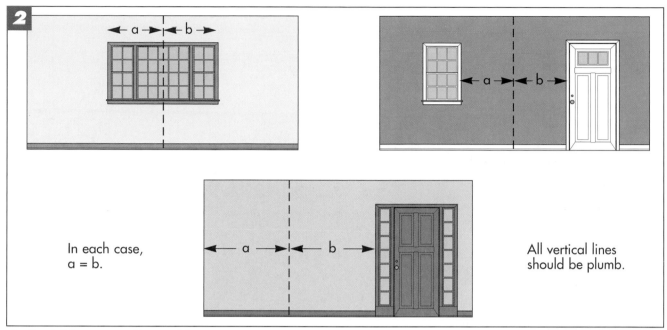

In each case,
a = b.

All vertical lines
should be plumb.

2. Establish a center line and lay out.

On a large wall, it is usually best to start the layout with a vertical line somewhere near the middle. If a single obstruction, such as a wall or a window, is reasonably centered in the room, then draw a line through its center. With two obstructions, make your center line at the middle of the distance between their inside edges. If you have a single offset obstruction, divide the unobstructed portion of the wall in half.

Then add a horizontal line to divide the wall into four quadrants. Add reference lines to separate the field tiles from any trim tiles. Use a carpenter's level to establish vertical and horizontal reference lines.

On a wall that is less than 8 feet wide, you may want to make sure that the cut tiles on either side are close to the same size. The only way to ensure this is to make a complete dry run of one horizontal course.

EXPERTS' INSIGHT

EXTENDING ELECTRICAL BOXES

When tiling around electrical outlets and switches, remove the cover plates and set tile right up to the cutout in the wall. This may mean that you will have to move the electrical box out, so that it will be flush with the finished tile surface. Extension rings are available at electrical supply outlets; mount them on the existing boxes. Before you begin tiling, make sure that you can find extension rings in the size you need, or talk to an electrician about other options.

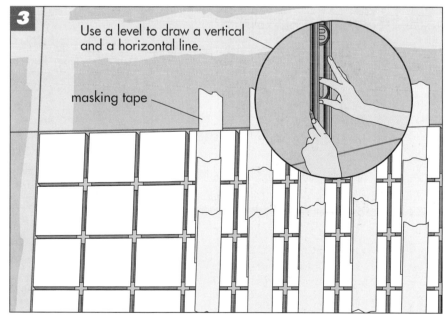

Use a level to draw a vertical and a horizontal line.

masking tape

3. Hold the tiles in place.

Gravity works against you when installing wall tiles. Usually wall tile adhesive is sticky enough so that the tiles will not fall off, and most wall tiles are self-spaced, so they will not slide down. In a more difficult installation, you may have to use spacers to keep the tiles from slipping, and masking tape to hold them on the wall. On each column of tiles, affix tape that is taut and well-adhered to the wall tile while the adhesive cures.

COPING WITH OBSTRUCTIONS

A careful do-it-yourselfer can usually produce professional-looking results when tiling a flat, unobstructed wall. Handling those not-so-flat walls full of obstructions is, obviously, more difficult. Plan carefully where your project entails working around obstacles or turning corners. Learning how to anticipate such disruptions is a necessary component of every installation. Wherever you can, avoid obstructions. And prepare for tackling obstructions you can't ignore. Practice cutting and trimming on scraps or extra tiles so when you're cutting tiles to fit around real obstructions, you'll be ready.

RIGHT: If a window is set in a deep recess, consider tiling the sill and perhaps the sides as well. A tiled window surround makes an ideal setting for potted plants.

ABOVE: *Sometimes obstructions create opportunities for interesting designs. Rather than tiling the entire wall behind this stove (and having to make cutouts for receptacles) this angled arrangement bypasses them.*

ABOVE: *Installing tile in a bathroom will often involve working around existing plumbing supplies, drains, and fixtures. Sometimes you can handle the problem by dismantling the plumbing, cutting or drilling a* hole in the tile before installing it (see page 35), and then replacing the plumbing after the tile is in place. Other times, you must work around the plumbing, notching the tile as needed (see page 41).

RIGHT: Electrical fixtures, receptacles, and switches like the ones in this bathroom are common obstructions that look deceptively easy to work around. The main difficulty is extending the metal or plastic fixture, switch, or receptacle box so it is flush with the finished tile surface. Purchase easy-to-install box extenders for the electrical box. Once these are in place, trim tile to wrap around the box (see page 41).

BELOW: Major appliances such as this commercial-grade cooktop and vent take special planning. Manufacturer's specs are helpful, but there is no substitute for having the unit itself on hand to confirm measurements when tiling. Plan your installation so the cooktop can be readily removed without damaging the tile.

ABOVE: Corners are the most commonly encountered obstruction in tiling. Lay out your job carefully so the horizontal grout joints on adjacent walls are aligned. Outside corners are vulnerable to damage. Plastic trim pieces can be used to protect the edge.

TILING A WINDOW RECESS

A tiled window recess won't rot, will resist water stains, and won't get scratched by cats seeking a sunny refuge. Plain terra-cotta tiles are an attractive choice; decorative, handpainted tiles can add a splash of color. If the surrounding wall is tiled, incorporate the window recess into the larger project. Use bullnose tiles or special windowsill tiles to round the edges. It is usually best to tile the recess after the wall, so that the recess tiles can overlap the wall tile. In a tub surround with a window, cut down on maintenance problems by replacing sashes with glass block and then tiling the recess.

YOU'LL NEED

TIME: Less than a day of labor, but allow a day for the adhesive to cure before grouting.
SKILLS: Careful removal of molding, setting wall tile.
TOOLS: Flat pry bar, tiling and grouting tools.

EXPERTS' INSIGHT

TILE AS TRIM

Tile is most often used to cover fairly broad areas; it makes for a wall that is low in maintenance as well as attractive. Sometimes, however, tile can make a stunning impact when it is used for small accents. One excellent example: Wood casing trim around doors and windows serves to hide an unattractive gap between materials. Tile can perform that function just as well, and with a good deal more pizzazz, especially if you choose decorative trim tiles.

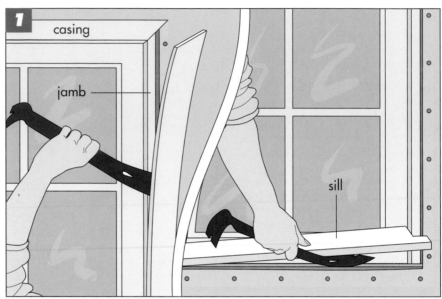

1. Remove molding and sill.
Remove the window casing, then pry off the sill. You may need to cut the sill to get it out. Now examine the jamb, and decide how far inward toward the window the tile will extend. If the window has stop molding, decide whether to leave it in place or remove it. You can tile directly on top of the jamb, or install backerboard first.

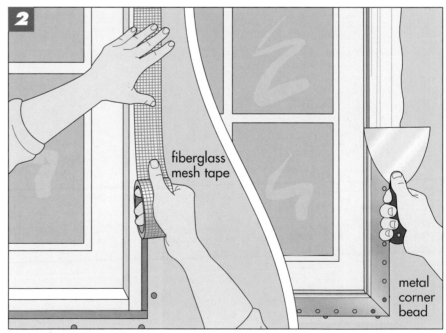

2. Prepare the wall.
Stuff the gap with fiberglass insulation if none exists; take care on an old window not to hinder the movement of the weights that are attached by ropes to the sashes. If you will be tiling the wall, apply fiberglass mesh joint tape, and fill in with joint compound. Allow to dry, apply a second coat, and sand smooth. If you will be painting the wall, carefully install metal outside corner bead, apply joint compound, and sand. Sand the jamb as well.

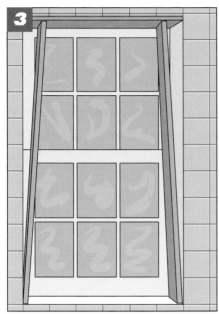

3. Support top pieces.

Install any wall tiles flush to the jamb, so you will have a consistent grout line at the corners (see right). Make a support system using three boards to hold the ceiling tiles in place. Allow them to set before continuing.

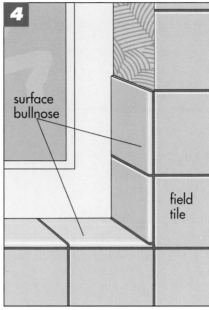

surface bullnose

field tile

4. Set the tiles.

Set tiles in adhesive and grout the same as for a standard wall installation. Use bullnose for a tiled wall (as shown) or for a painted wall. Or, use one of the other options pictured below.

5. Caulk the window.

Take special care to completely caulk the joint between the tile and the window; you don't want all your work to be destroyed in a few years by water damage.

Other corner options.

Another option for tiling a recess uses surface bullnose tiles on the wall to overlap the tiles on the recess (left). Or use corner edging tiles similar to V-cap tiles

used on countertops, but without the raised lip (above center); install the edging pieces before tiling the recess. For a decorative touch, apply a border strip around the recess (right).

Install bullnose pieces in the recess so they cap the border strips, or butt field tiles up to the border pieces if they have a finished edge.

TILING COUNTERTOPS

Tile countertops are durable and offer a wide range of color and texture options that can make them an attractive design feature. However, be sure to address a few drawbacks: Tile is much more prone to break dropped glasses and dishes than are other countertop surfaces. Also, grout is easily stained and can be tough to clean, even when coated with a grout sealer. Choose colors and materials that will enhance performance, and keep the countertop clean and well maintained. Dark-colored glazes are more likely to show scratches than light-colored glazes. Glazed, vitreous, or impervious tiles do the best job of resisting moisture and stains. Unglazed tiles should be used only on countertops that will remain dry.

ABOVE: For a band of dramatic color and a practical surface, run your countertop tile up onto the backsplash. Use tile, adhesive, and grout that can withstand the moisture. *Install the tiles over a membrane and backerboard (see pages 26–28) to assure that your project will withstand the hard use a kitchen countertop demands.*

EXPERTS' INSIGHT

TILE SELECTIVELY

Some people don't want to consider tile for countertop use, at least in the kitchen, because of its hard surface and the difficulty of keeping grout joints clean. However, you can use tile and avoid most of these problems by being selective. Don't install tile on the major food preparation surfaces in the kitchen. Instead, match the material used on the surface with the function of the countertop. Plastic laminate, for example, might be preferred around the sink and food preparation area, while tile can cover other countertops in the kitchen. Or save the tile for use as a backsplash.

ABOVE: One of the distinct pleasures of tiling a bathroom is that you can show your free-spirited side. Experiment with playful colors and bold patterns that you wouldn't even think about using in any other room. *Make a small bathroom feel larger by using a lot of contrast, or give the room a unified sense by sticking to a single color throughout.*

ABOVE: Tile has always been more popular in the bathroom than in the kitchen because you don't have to worry about the aesthetic and hygienic effects of food and grease spills, or breaking fragile dishes on the hard surface. In addition, because tile is so often used elsewhere in the bath, it makes sense to use it on the countertop as well.

RIGHT: There are advantages to using tile around a cooktop. Heat generated by the burners will not affect the tiles, and most tiles won't be damaged if you place a hot pan on them. Often it makes sense to use tile around the cooktop and use other surfacing materials for countertops in washup and food preparation areas.

LAYING OUT COUNTERTOPS

Countertops are hardworking, high-visibility surfaces worthy of close attention to detail. Small misalignments can grow in magnitude as the job goes on, so take the time to get the layout exactly the way you want it. Most countertops are small enough that you can do a complete dry run with loose tiles before installation. Try to place equal-sized cut tiles along the sides and back of the countertop. If a back wall is uneven, make the adjustment there, not along the front edge.

YOU'LL NEED

TIME: A day and a half to install substrate and tile.
SKILLS: Measuring and marking a layout; cutting and attaching plywood.
TOOLS: Drill, level, square, circular saw or sabersaw.

1. Install a plywood surface.
The countertop substrate should be at least one layer of ¾-inch plywood. Take care that the front edges are square and parallel to the walls. Make the whole top perfectly level. Attach with construction adhesive and screws.

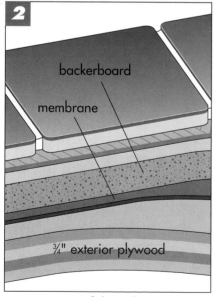

2. Waterproof the substrate.
For a fully waterproofed installation, add a waterproofing membrane (15-pound felt paper or 4-mil polyethylene) followed by backerboard. Seal the joints of the backerboard with fiberglass-mesh tape, filled with thin-set mortar.

3. Lay out the job.
When laying out an L-shaped countertop, start at the inside corner, and plan to use full tiles there. Align field tiles with the edge of the substrate unless you plan to use edging trim tiles, in which case draw a reference line separating trim from field tiles. (See page 77 for edging options.) If possible, plan so that grout lines will be evenly spaced from the sides of the sink. Run cut tiles around to the back edges, along the backsplash.

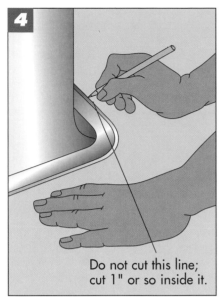

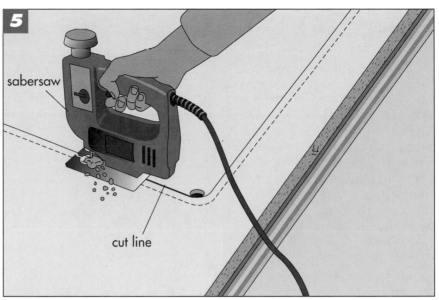

Do not cut this line;
cut 1" or so inside it.

sabersaw

cut line

4. Mark the sink cutout.

Determine where the sink can fit into your sink base cabinet. Flip the sink upside down and trace the outline. Remove the sink and draw a cut line an inch or so inside the outline. Some new sinks come with a paper template that can be used instead.

5. Cut the hole.

You could simply cut the opening with a circular saw, starting with a plunge cut, but cutting through backerboard with a circular saw will make a huge cloud of dust. So use a sabersaw instead. Drill holes just inside the cut line at each corner. Use a drill bit large enough to match the radius of the sink corners. Use a sabersaw equipped with a rough-cutting blade to cut the sink opening; have extra blades on hand. Install the sink before or after tiling, depending on the type (see below).

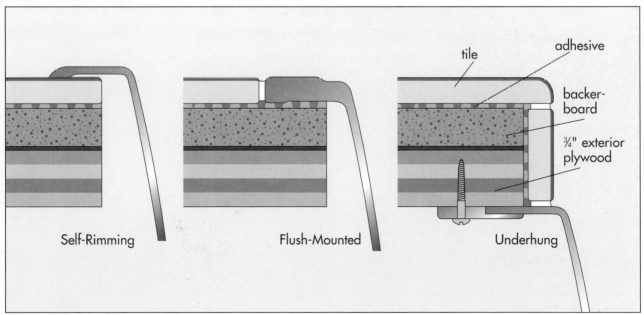

tile

adhesive

backer-
board

¾" exterior
plywood

Self-Rimming

Flush-Mounted

Underhung

Sink Options.

If your countertop tiling project involves a sink, be sure to buy the sink and learn how it is installed before you set any tile. The most common type of kitchen sink is self-rimming. Install it after the countertop has been tiled; the edges of the sink rest on top of the tile. Install a flush-mounted sink before tiling, and run the tile up to the edge of the sink. Underhung sinks are difficult to install, but perform well. Flush-mounted and underhung sinks don't have a lip, so anything on the countertop can be wiped directly into the sink.

SETTING TILE COUNTERTOPS

Choose tiles made for the purpose. They should be glazed, or they will stain easily. It is usually best to use either a light-colored grout or one that comes close to the color of the tile, rather than a dark, starkly contrasting color that will emphasize any imperfections.

To be sure the tile color and finish are consistent, work with a tile dealer who can supply you with all of the field tiles; decorative, sink cap, or surface bullnose tiles for the front edge; and surface bullnose or radius cap for the backsplash. Every tile whose edge will be exposed must have a rounded edge on one side called a bullnose or cap. Don't use a field tile and then attempt to give it a finished edge with grout; it will look ugly and wear poorly.

Choose the adhesive recommended by your dealer. Thin-set mortar is usually the best choice. If you want to make the installation waterproof, be sure to choose all materials with that end in mind.

Work slowly and systematically. Setting a tile countertop is an ideal weekend project, and provides good training for tackling larger or more complex tiling jobs later.

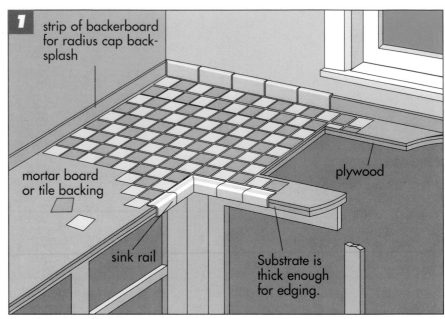

1. Plan the job.
Prepare a firm, level, and flat surface for the tiles. Be sure that the total thickness of the substrate will be covered by the edging you choose (see next page). Check the substrate for level and square. If you are using backsplash edging tile with a large radius, provide backing for it by fastening a strip of backerboard to the wall (see page 78). Check the layout for the backsplash to find out if you will encounter any obstructions.

YOU'LL NEED

TIME: A full day to install about 12 feet of countertop, plus 2–3 hours the following day for grouting and cleaning.
SKILLS: Laying out, spreading adhesive, cutting, installing, and grouting tile.
TOOLS: Tape measure, level, square, tile cutter, notched trowel, grout float.

2. Lay out a dry run.
Set the tiles in place, positioning them exactly as you want the finished surface to look. Use plastic spacers, and check that all lines are straight. To mark lines for cutting, hold each tile in place rather than measuring (page 43).

EXPERTS' INSIGHT

THE RIGHT GROUT
Because grout joints on countertops are visible and subjected to spills, it is important to use the best grout mixture possible. Use sanded grout for grout joints wider than 1/16 inch. Mix the grout with a liquid latex additive rather than water for added protection against liquid penetration. If mildew is likely to be a problem, use an additive that inhibits the growth of mildew. Plan to seal the grout a week or two after installation.

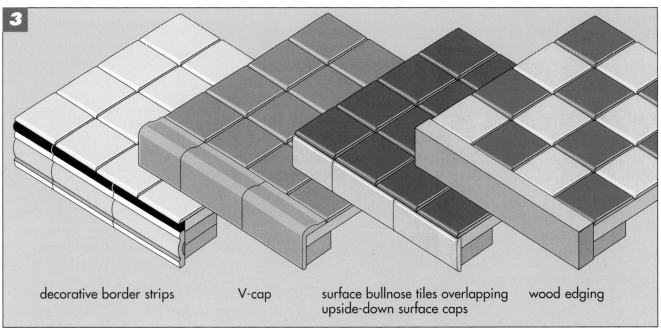

3

decorative border strips   V-cap   surface bullnose tiles overlapping   wood edging
                                                  upside-down surface caps

3. Choose the edging.

The edging on a countertop is not just a decorative element added on at the end of the job. As an integral part of the counter, it must figure in your planning at each step of the way. Your choice of edge treatment will affect preparation and thickness of the substrate as well as the placement of reference lines.

You can add color and interest to a countertop by edging it with a combination of decorative border strips overlapped by surface bullnose tiles. A V-cap provides a slight lip that keeps water from dripping down the edge of the counter. Another alternative involves two bullnose edging pieces, one on the counter surface, one on the edging. Install the edge pieces and the surface tiles at the same time to keep them aligned.

EDGING WITH WOOD

Wood looks great as an edging material on kitchen countertops, and it is easy to install. It does create some additional maintenance concerns, however. Wood expands and contracts with temperature and humidity changes, but tile and grout do not. So keep the wood separated from the tile with caulk. Set the edging flush with the top of the tile, or a little higher to create a drip-proof lip. Position the tiles about ⅛ inch shy of the edge of the substrate to allow space for caulk. Attach the edging to the plywood substrate with countersunk screws every 6 to 8 inches, then hide the screw heads with plugs or filler. Or attach the edging with a biscuit joiner, for a surface free of screw holes.

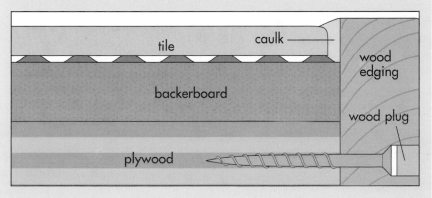

tile — caulk
backerboard
wood edging
wood plug
plywood

CAUTION!

SEAL THE WOOD
One of the biggest challenges posed by wood edging on a countertop is keeping the wood looking as good as new years after it was installed. Use a tough hardwood, such as maple or oak, to help minimize dents and scrapes. Before installing the edging, coat all sides with a durable clear wood finish such as polyurethane. Apply more finish to any penetrations made in the wood while it is being installed. In the years to come, watch for dark stains on the wood, which could indicate that water has found its way into the wood. In that case, sand away the stain and apply another coat of finish.

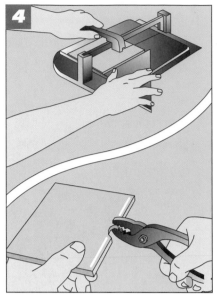

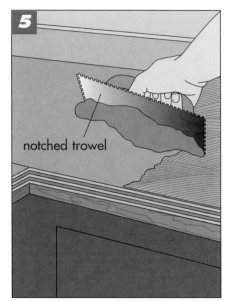

notched trowel

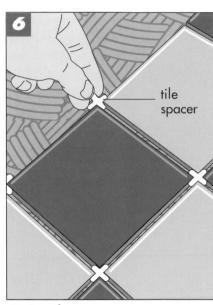

tile spacer

4. Cut tiles.

For the straight cuts, use a snap cutter. If you have many cuts to make, a wet saw may make the job go faster. Many of the cuts will be for the same size, so you can set the guide and cut them factory-style. For small curved or irregular cuts, use nippers or a rod saw. See pages 40–41 for instructions.

5. Spread adhesive.

Mix the thin-set mortar as directed on the label. If the powder does not contain a latex additive, use a liquid additive instead of water to mix with the powder. Let the mixture rest for ten minutes, then mix it again. Spread the adhesive with a notched trowel.

6. Set tiles.

Set the tiles along the reference lines, pressing each one into the adhesive with a slight twist. Avoid sliding the tiles. Use plastic spacers to keep all of the joints even. Check the alignment of set tiles regularly.

BACKSPLASH OPTIONS

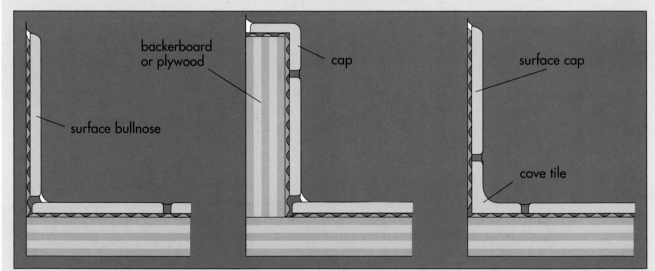

backerboard or plywood

cap

surface cap

surface bullnose

cove tile

Integrate the backsplash with the countertop, using the same tiles on both surfaces, with grout joints that line up. Or, treat the backsplash as an element all its own, using colors and sizes of tile that are unrelated to those on the countertop. Make colorful backsplashes by using a variety of tiles. If you are setting backsplash tiles directly on the wall, it must be reasonably flat and in sound condition. Use surface bullnose tiles. A built-up backsplash mimics the look of a traditional mortar-bed installation. Use plywood or backerboard to fill in the space behind a tile and cap. For easy cleanup, install a cove tile in the corner with a surface cap above it.

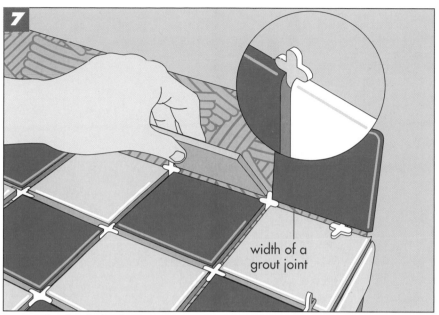

width of a grout joint

radius cap

7. Set backsplash tiles.

If you are using backsplash tiles that are the same width as the tiles on the countertop, install them so that the grout joints line up. Since these tiles are not subject to much wear and tear, it is possible to set them directly on the wall. Set backsplash tiles above the countertop tiles by the width of a grout joint.

8. Trim the backsplash.

If you use bullnose tiles set directly on the wall, you will not need to add trim tiles to the backsplash. If the backsplash is built out away from the wall, add radius cap tiles.

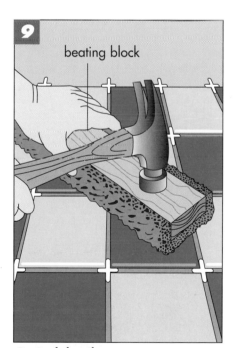

beating block

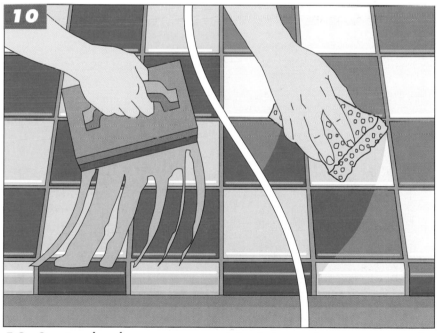

9. Bed the tiles.

After setting tiles in one section, bed them into the adhesive with a beating block. Move the beating block over the tiles while tapping lightly with a hammer. Clean out any excess adhesive that squeezes into grout joints.

10. Grout and seal.

Let the set tiles rest for 24 hours. Mix grout with a latex additive. Apply with a grout float, pushing the mixture into the joints. When the joints are filled, hold the float at nearly a right angle to the countertop and wipe away the excess. Do not use grout in the joint between the countertop and backsplash tiles; this joint and the space between the backsplash tile and the wall should be filled with caulk or sealant.

Wipe away excess grout with a sponge, then remove the grout haze once it appears. Apply grout sealer after the grout has cured.

TILING A BATHROOM SINKTOP

This project takes some time and patience, but the result can be a sinktop that adds an appealing custom touch to your makeover, melding the sink area with other tile surfaces in your bathroom.

Begin with an off-the-shelf cabinet base or, if you are an experienced woodworker, make one yourself. Select the sink, faucet, and grout at the same time as you buy your tiles, so you have a grouping that goes well together. Avoid choosing a pigmented grout of a color that contrasts strongly with the tiles.

YOU'LL NEED

TIME: A day to build the substrate and lay the tiles, another hour the next day to grout.
SKILLS: Building substrate, cutting and installing tiles.
TOOLS: Sabersaw, level, trowel, caulking gun, tiling tools.

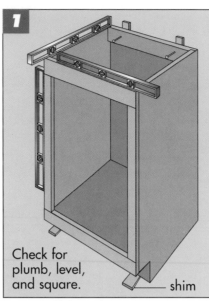

Check for plumb, level, and square. — shim

1. Install the cabinet.

If not already in place, install drain and supply lines. Cut holes in the back of the cabinet for the pipes, and slide in the cabinet. Shim at the floor and wall where necessary to ensure that the cabinet is plumb and level. Attach it to the wall by driving screws through the cabinet framing and into wall studs.

EXPERTS' INSIGHT

CHOOSING MATERIALS

■ Choose tiles that are made for the purpose; regular wall tiles will crack. The tiles you use should be ⅜- to ½-inch thick with a glazed surface. Buy all of the tiles at the same time—the regular field tiles as well as the bullnose tiles for the edges of the counter and the backsplash.

■ A vitreous china sink is a compatible choice because its surface has a texture similar to tile. Enameled cast iron is also a good choice. Be sure to select a self-rimming sink, so you can simply set it on top of the countertop and cover the rough edges of the cut tiles.

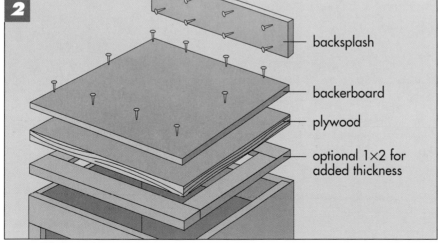

backsplash

backerboard

plywood

optional 1×2 for added thickness

2. Build the substrate.

The surface under your tiles must be perfectly flat and smooth, and the edges and backsplash should be properly sized to accommodate your arrangement of bullnose tiles. If you can, plan the size of the subsurface so that you'll use as many whole tiles as possible.

Cut ¾-inch plywood to the size needed. To thicken the substrate for tile edging, fasten 1×2 pieces around the perimeter of the cabinet with glue and screws. On top of the plywood, add a piece of backerboard. Attach it with screws, driving the heads just below the surface.

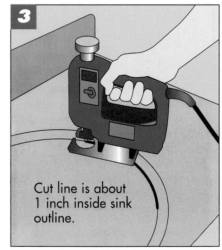

Cut line is about 1 inch inside sink outline.

3. Cut the hole.

The sink manufacturer may supply you with a template for marking the cutout. If not, center the sink upside-down on the top and draw an outline. Draw a second line about 1 inch inside the first, and cut that line with a sabersaw.

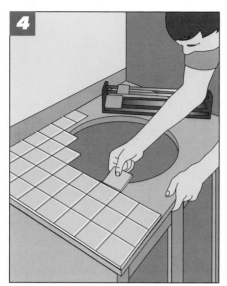

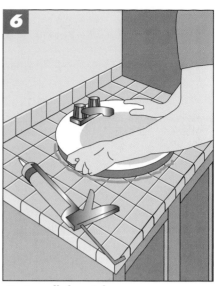

4. Make a dry run.

Lay the tiles out exactly where you want them, using plastic spacers for all the joints and cutting tiles where necessary. When setting down pieces at the perimeter, remember that the mortar behind the edging pieces will be about ⅛ inch thick. Hold the sink in place above the opening to make sure no tile edges will be visible.

5. Apply the adhesive.

Remove the tiles and place them in the order in which they will be adhered. Mix thin-set mortar and apply it with a notched trowel by first laying it on thickly, then combing it with the notches for a perfectly level surface. Give the tiles a little push as you place them. Use the spacers to maintain consistent joint lines.

6. Install the sink.

Grout the tiles, and allow the grout to dry. Set the sink in place, and make the plumbing connections. If the sink has mounting clips, install and tighten them; a heavy sink will not need them. Finish by running a bead of silicone caulk around the sink's rim. Smooth the caulk using a rag soaked with paint thinner.

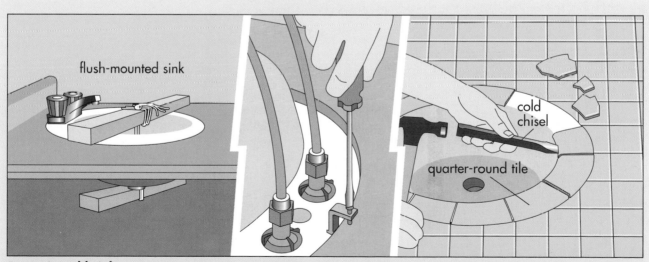

Removing old sinks.

Rimmed sinks are usually easy to remove: Unhook the plumbing connections, disconnect mounting clips (if any) from underneath, cut the bead of caulk, and pull up. Use a couple of pieces of 2×4 and a length of rope to support a flush-mounted sink as you remove the clamps

that hold it in place. Otherwise, it may fall down into the cabinet. A recessed sink, which sits under the countertop surface—usually tiled—is held with special mounting clamps. If they are rusted, use penetrating oil to help loosen them before unscrewing. If you cannot turn the countertop upside down as

shown, be sure to support the sink as you remove it.

If you want to keep your tiles and your new sink is large enough, carefully chip away the old quarter-round tiles that cover the top of a recessed sink. Then install a rimmed sink that covers the opening and install new quarter round.

TILING SHOWERS AND TUBS

Perhaps nowhere else in the house other than the bathroom does tile so successfully unite beauty and functionality. Properly installed, tile can resist all the water you can throw at it. With so many colors, sizes, and patterns available, you are almost guaranteed to find a design that satisfies all of your needs. And when it comes time for cleanup, tile will demand less of your time than just about any other material that you can imagine. Perhaps best of all, it has never been easier for a nonprofessional to accomplish professional-looking results. The secret to a long-lasting shower and tub installation is taking the extra effort to make the surface waterproof, and performing the routine maintenance required to keep it that way.

RIGHT: Few materials other than tile could successfully wrap the raised floor, built-in seat, and window of this custom, jumbo-sized shower area.

BELOW: Tile accommodates the custom profile of this corner bath, neatly merging with the glass block accents on the step.

RIGHT: Tile is a natural material for waterproofing awkward spaces. In this bathroom, tile helps transform an under-the-eaves corner into a unified and functional bathing area. Decorative tile helps soften the look while allowing plenty of latitude for decorating schemes in the future.

BELOW: An abundance of contrast is not necessary to achieve a good design. Often, one or two simple design elements are all that is required to give character and definition to a room. Here, a subtle color pattern on the floor and some light detailing on the tub surround do the job. When a simple design is what you seek, try to establish a theme and carry it through the entire project.

TILING A TUB SURROUND

*I*n a tub that also contains a shower, plan to install tile from the top of the tub to about 6 inches above the showerhead. If the tub doesn't have a shower, tile at least one foot above the tub (more if you anticipate a lot of splashing). If you want to tile the ceiling as well, use a fast-setting adhesive; it will hold the tiles in place without support. (Install ceiling tile so that it doesn't have to line up with the wall tiles—say, diagonally—because getting it to fit will be very difficult. If an end wall continues out past the tub, continue the tiles at least one full vertical row beyond the tub, and run it down to the floor. Use surface bullnose tiles for the edges.

Set the tile on a backerboard substrate (see pages 36–37 for information on backerboard). The backerboard itself should be installed over a waterproofing membrane of 15-pound felt paper or 4-mil polyethylene. Overlay the edges of the membrane and seal the seams of the backerboard with fiberglass mesh tape bedded in adhesive.

If you have a window with wood casing and jambs, consider tearing it out or cutting back the casing and tiling the recess (pages 70–71). You may wish to eliminate the problems of a wood window altogether by installing glass block.

YOU'LL NEED

TIME: A day to prepare the substrate, most of a day to tile, and a few hours to grout.
SKILLS: Cutting and installing backerboard, patching walls, cutting and installing tile.
TOOLS: Drill, hole saw, scraping tool, wall patching tools, level, a straight board, notched trowel, snap cutter, nibbler, hacksaw with rod saw, grouting float.

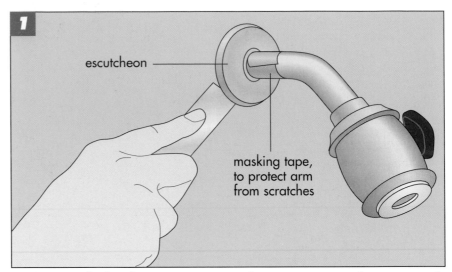

1. Remove the hardware.
You don't want to cut tiles to fit precisely around hardware. Pry the shower-arm escutcheon away from the wall, and perhaps remove the shower arm as well. Remove the tub spout; most can be unscrewed by sticking the handle of a screwdriver or hammer in the spout and turning counterclockwise. Remove the faucet handles and escutcheons.

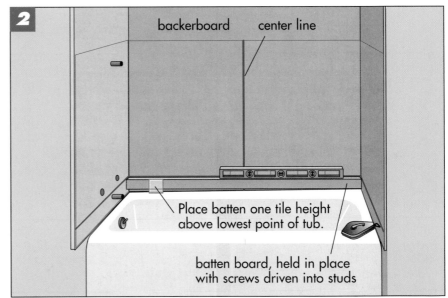

2. Prepare and lay out.
The walls must be solid, and at least close to plumb and square (see page 31). If necessary, remove the existing substrate and install a waterproofing membrane and backerboard. Be sure that the new surface is flush with any adjoining surface.

Establish a vertical reference line by laying the tiles in a row on the tub and making sure you will either have the same size tile on each end, or that you will not have any very narrow pieces. If the end walls are out of square with the rear wall, factor in how the pieces will change in size as you move upward. Establish a horizontal reference line, measuring from the low point of the tub if it is not level, and tack a very straight batten board along its length.

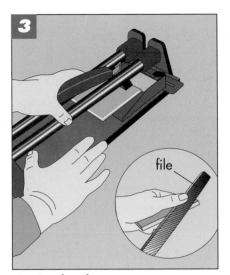

3. Cut the tile.
Use a snap cutter for the straight cuts. Hold the tile in place and mark it for cutting. Align it on the cutter, score the surface by pushing down while sliding the cutter once across the tile, then push down on the handle. For a series of cuts of the same size, use the adjustable guide. Smooth the ragged cut edges with a rubbing stone or file.

4. Set the tile.
Apply adhesive with a notched trowel, taking care not to cover your layout lines. Set the tiles, giving each a little twist and pushing to make sure it sticks. Start with the row sitting on the batten. Most wall tiles are self-spacing. Once you have several rows installed, remove the batten and install the bottom row.

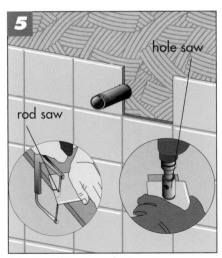

5. Cut tile around pipes.
Cuts around pipes usually do not have to be precise since the opening is covered with an escutcheon. Use a nibbler to eat away at a curved cut, or a hacksaw equipped with a rod-saw blade. To cut a hole, use a tile-cutting hole saw. Or, set the tile on a piece of scrap wood, drill a series of closely spaced holes with a masonry bit, and tap out the hole.

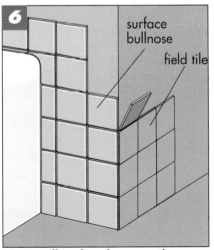

6. Install end and corner tiles.
Cut the curved piece at the corner of the tub with a rod saw; it may take several attempts to get it just right. Use surface bullnose tiles everywhere there is an exposed edge. (Do not use a field tile edged with grout—it will look very sloppy and won't wear well.)

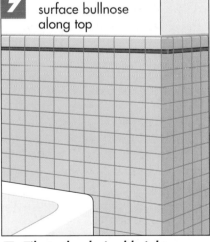

7. Tile to the desired height.
When you reach the top row, wipe away excess adhesive from the wall as you install surface bullnose tiles. Use outside corner pieces (*down angles*), which have two cap edges, on all outside corners.

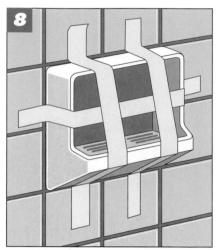

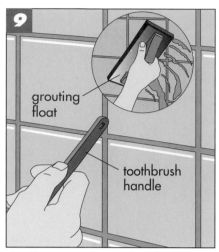

8. Attach ceramic accessories.
Apply adhesive and use masking tape to hold soap dishes and other accessories in place until they are set. Take the tape off after a day or two and apply grout, but wait a week or so before using.

9. Grout, caulk, and seal.
Mix the grout with latex additive, and push it into the joints with a grouting float held nearly flat. Tip the float up and wipe away the excess. Carefully wipe the surface to produce consistent grout lines. Use a toothbrush handle or other tool to shape the joints. Caulk the corners and edges. Wipe and dry-buff the haze.

10. Reattach the hardware.
Reattach the plumbing hardware. If you need to install a shower arm, use a thin tool handle to tighten it. If the new tile has caused valves or nipples to be recessed too far and you can't install a faucet or spout, visit a plumbing supplier and pick up suitable extensions. Once the grout has cured, apply sealer.

TILING AN ACCESS PANEL

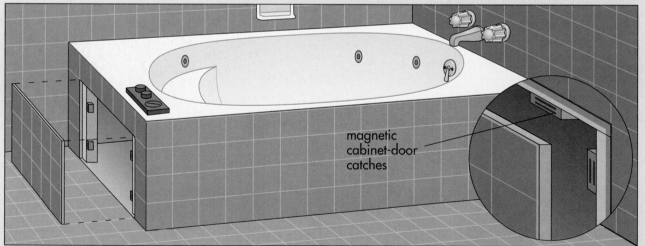

Plumbing access panels are usually located in an adjoining room, but yours might be in the bathroom. The panel may have been installed when the bathroom was built, or it might have been built out of necessity when a plumber needed to gain access to the pipes and valves supplying the tub. Don't just tile over the panel, because a plumber may need to get in there again. The easiest solution is to cover the panel with a piece of plastic, well-painted plywood, or a plastic access panel made for the purpose (available at home centers).

Or, make a tiled access panel. Cut a piece of plywood sized to hold full tiles. Install tiles on it so they will align with the surrounding tiles, and trim the edges with painted wood molding; drive screws through the molding to hold the panel in place. Or skip the molding, and attach with magnetic cabinet door catches, as shown above.

TILING A SHOWER STALL

If you are building a new shower stall, the easiest approach is to install a prefabricated shower pan, and then tile above it. (A shower *pan,* or base, is the shower's floor, with a hole for the drain.) Several types of pans are available, and they are all fairly easy to install (see page 88). If you want the floor of the shower to be tiled as well, look for a pan that can be tiled over.

A 36-inch-square shower stall (the size is determined by the size of the pan) will be comfortable for adults; a 32-incher will feel cramped. If a vented drain and water supply lines do not exist, you will need to install them. Consult with or hire a plumber; it is especially important that the drain be properly vented.

Don't place the shower in a corner of the bathroom just to save work; framing new walls is a fairly small part of the job. Rather than tiling over existing walls that aren't plumb and square, start with plumb, square walls and it will be much easier to achieve a professional-looking tile job.

Use surface bullnose tiles where the edge of a tile will be visible, and corner pieces (*down angles*) where two edges will be visible. Decide exactly where you want the tiles to stop. For example, you may want to wrap tile around the thickness of the walls where the shower door will be installed.

YOU'LL NEED

TIME: One day to install a shower pan and substrate, another day to tile, and a few hours to grout.
SKILLS: Framing walls, cutting and installing backerboard and tile, grouting.
TOOLS: Drill, circular saw, level, tiling and grouting tools.

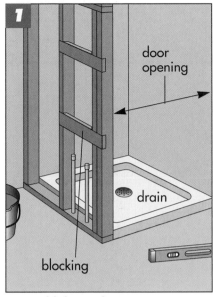

1. Build the enclosure.
Decide if you want to install a glass shower door or hang a curtain, and whether you want walls up to the ceiling or not. Build a 2×4 frame, plumb and square to adjoining walls, with blocking to support the plumbing.

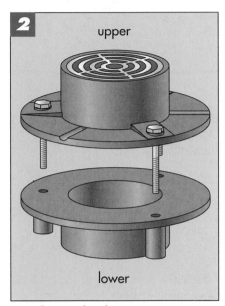

2. Choose the drain.
The drain for most shower pans is a two-piece unit, usually made of cast iron or brass. Choose a drain that matches both your pan and the existing drain line. Ask your dealer to show you how to attach it to the pan and to the drain line.

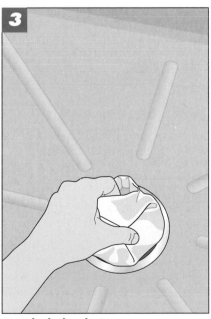

3. Block the drain.
Before you begin preparing the substrate or tiling, block the drain with a rag. Better yet, tape a thick piece of plastic over the opening to keep out debris, which could seriously clog the drain.

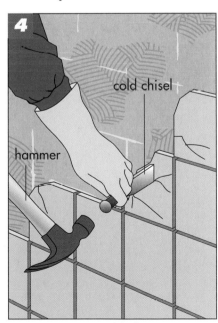

4. Remove any old tile.
If you need to remove old tile first, remove as much of the grout surrounding the tiles as possible, then use a hammer and cold chisel to knock out the tiles. Wear eye protection and gloves.

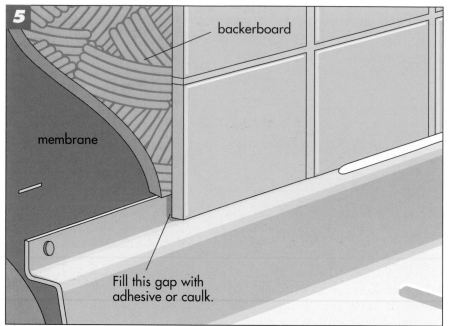

5

backerboard

membrane

Fill this gap with adhesive or caulk.

5. Install the pan.

Set the pan in place, and check it for level in both directions; shim if necessary. Attach the drain to the pan and to the drain line, and test by pouring buckets of water down the drain. Most pans have a flange that fits tightly against the wall; you will install the backerboard slightly above the bottom curve of the flange.

SHOWER PAN OPTIONS

Shower pans are fabricated out of fiberglass, acrylic, terrazzo, or other materials. These pans cannot be tiled. Buy the best quality that you can afford. Thin, flimsy products may not last, since con-stant flexing in the pan can create leaks. And study the installation instructions of the pan before you buy it—sturdier, heavier models may require less work to install. In addition to a standard square shape, consider a larger pan with a seat or two, or a pentagonal shape (which typically is used with a three-sided glass door.)

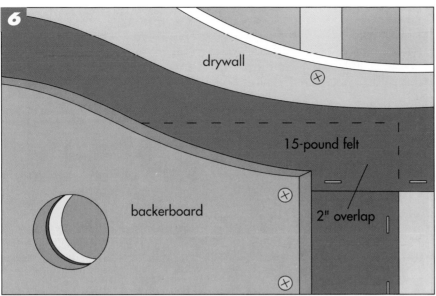

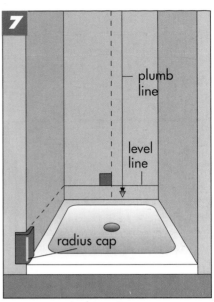

6. Prepare the substrate.

Install the waterproofing membrane: Staple or nail 15-pound felt paper or 4-mil polyethylene to the studs (or drywall). Overlap upper sections of the membrane over the lower sections by at least 2 inches. Cut and install backerboard. Drill holes for the shower valves and spouts with a carbide-tipped hole saw. Attach with screws driven into studs. Keep the backerboard about ¼ inch above the shower pan, and fill the gap with silicone caulk or tile adhesive. Cover joints with fiberglass mesh tape and seal with tile adhesive.

7. Layout for the tiles.

Carefully mark horizontal and vertical reference lines. Make sure you will not end up with small slivers of tiles in the corners, and avoid having different-sized tiles on either side of a wall. Make sure your radius cap or trim tiles will fit properly along the edges.

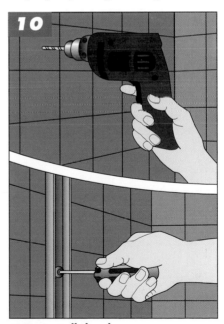

8. Set the tiles.

Apply tile adhesive with a notched trowel. Don't cover over your reference lines. Use a batten board (pages 84–85). Give each tile a little twist as you push it into place. Wipe away any excess adhesive immediately. Allow to set at least a day before grouting.

9. Install the finish plumbing.

After the grout has dried, slide on the escutcheons and install faucet handle or handles and the showerhead. Make sure the area around the handle is well sealed; if your unit does not have a rubber gasket that grabs tightly to the wall, apply a bead of silicone caulk.

10. Install the door.

Mark hole locations to mount the door frame or the curtain-rod holders. Carefully drill through the tiles with a masonry bit. Apply silicone caulk to the back of the frame, and attach it by driving screws into a stud or into plastic anchors. Caulk the inside edges.

RENEWING A FIREPLACE WITH TILE

As houses are remodeled and updated, often the style of the fireplace gets overlooked. And after years of use a hearth and fireplace surround can become stained and damaged. Refacing a fireplace surround is not a difficult project, as long as the floor and wall are solid and in good repair. By investing a weekend and purchasing a small amount of tiles, you can add a striking touch to your living room.

Have your fireplace and chimney inspected and cleaned before you begin. A beautified fireplace is not necessarily a safe fireplace, and a simple refacing cannot cure any internal problems.

RIGHT: This eye-catching fireplace uses a sophisticated combination of tiles covering everything but the mantlepiece. Though not a project for beginners, it demonstrates the power of a few well-chosen decorative tiles.

ABOVE: The use of stone tiles like these handsome slates are a traditional choice for fireplace hearths and surrounds. In addition, consider granite, marble, and brick veneer, and for hearths, flagstone.

ABOVE: Use color and tile size to allow the fireplace to blend in with, or stand apart from, the room. The deep terra-cotta tones of these tiles are neutral enough to fit any color scheme of future decorating plans. The raised hearth helps radiate fireplace heat at seating level where it is of the most benefit. This is an ideal place to use tile.

TILING AROUND A FIREPLACE

Before beginning any remodeling project involving a fireplace, check your local building codes for any requirements regarding the need for fire-resistant materials between the tile and a combustible wall. You may need to keep combustible materials, such as a mantel shelf, a specified distance from the firebox. The fireplace, damper, and chimney must be in good working condition, and the chimney should draw smoke out of the house easily. If the chimney has not been cleaned lately, have it inspected and cleaned before you begin setting tile.

If the existing surface around your fireplace is cracked or loose, consult with a professional before proceeding. Removing an old fireplace surround often entails disrupting the existing firebox and chimney, and that should not be done by an amateur.

YOU'LL NEED

TIME: About one day to install the tile, once the surface has been prepared.
SKILLS: Laying out, cutting, and installing floor and wall tile.
TOOLS: Notched trowel, rubber mallet, tile cutter, drill, hammer, grouting float, sponge.

CAUTION!

*HEAT-RESISTANT MATERIALS
The heat generated by a fireplace can destroy the bond of many adhesives. Organic mastics and some thin-set mortars should not be used near a fireplace. Use only tiles and adhesives specifically made for heated surfaces.*

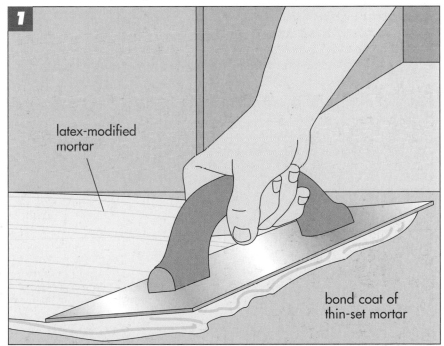

latex-modified mortar

bond coat of thin-set mortar

1. Prepare the surface.
Treat the existing surface as you would any other substrate. Clean off all soot and dirt. Remove any high spots with a rubbing stone or sanding block. Vacuum thoroughly. If the surface is not flat enough for setting tiles, coat it with a thin layer of thin-set mortar, and then create a level surface with latex-modified mortar. Take care when laying out the installation around the fireplace opening. Here it would look best to have full tiles. Adjust the location of the tiles horizontally or vertically to minimize the need for cutting. If you have trouble with the layout, consider using smaller tiles.

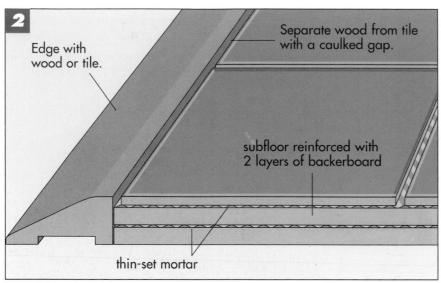

2 Edge with wood or tile.

Separate wood from tile with a caulked gap.

subfloor reinforced with 2 layers of backerboard

thin-set mortar

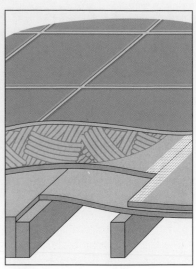

2. Tile the hearth.

If the hearth is surrounded by wood flooring, leave a gap around the perimeter the same width as the grout joints. Fill this gap with caulk or sealant once the tile has been grouted. The hearth is less affected by heat than the wall surround, but it must be strong enough to withstand firewood being dropped—and perhaps chopped—on it. If the existing hearth is less than 1⅛-inch thick, consider adding backerboard to strengthen the setting bed. If possible, use two layers of backerboard; bond them together and to the subfloor with thin-set mortar. Let the substrate cure for a couple of days, then set tiles.

Extending a raised hearth
To expand a raised hearth (found in some older homes), build a frame with 2×4s, plywood, and backerboard. Rip the 2×4s to the correct width, drill pilot holes, and screw them to the floor.

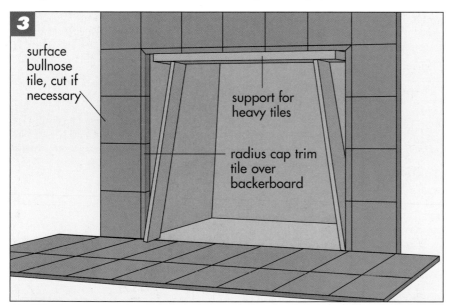

3 surface bullnose tile, cut if necessary

support for heavy tiles

radius cap trim tile over backerboard

3. Tile the surround.

Since the surround is exposed to high temperatures, use only materials that are heat resistant. The surround is frequently composed of a single row of large tiles around the opening, trimmed with molding on the sides and butting up against a mantel at the top. Consider trimming the surround with decorative tiles. Attach a 1×2 batten across the top of the fireplace to support the top horizontal row of tiles. Leave the batten in place for about 24 hours, giving the adhesive time to set. If you are installing large, heavy tiles, you will have better luck building a larger support out of three pieces of scrap lumber.

EXPERTS' INSIGHT

HEARTH MAINTENANCE

■ Tile is not indestructible, and marble, which is often used for hearths, is easy to scratch and stain. So don't abuse your hearth. Keep the grout well sealed to avoid stains from sooty wood. Buy and use a good grate or set of glass doors to keep sparks contained. And don't use your fireplace unless it is drawing well, or soot and smoke could get into your house.

■ Many fireplace hearths are too small to offer adequate protection to the floor. When installing new tile, go ahead and add another course or two, so you won't have to worry about sparks singeing your wood floor or carpeting.

INSTALLING A WOODSTOVE SURROUND

A woodstove radiates heat in all directions, so you must place it on a noncombustible surface and protect nearby walls. Follow local building codes and the manufacturer's recommendations for the stove's best location, and the size of the noncombustible hearth and fire wall. And check with your insurance agent to make sure your homeowner's insurance covers a woodstove.

Use tile or brick veneer. Also known as *thin brick,* brick veneer can be set much like tile, using thin-set mortar. Or look for a ceramic tile that mimics the appearance of brick. Run the flue pipe before installing the tile.

YOU'LL NEED

TIME: About one day to install the tile once the walls, chimney flue, and floor are prepared.
SKILLS: Laying out, cutting, and installing tile.
TOOLS: Hammer, tape measure, level, screwdriver, drill, tiling and grouting tools.

EXPERTS' INSIGHT

SAFE INSTALLATION OF A WOOD-BURNING STOVE

Modern wood-burning stoves are highly efficient, burning logs completely and sending little heat up the chimney. Follow the manufacturer's installation instructions carefully. Use a masonry chimney or a class-A metal flue. Be sure the chimney is high enough above the roof to draw well. Clean the flue regularly; burning wood produces creosote, which accumulates in the flue, creating a fire hazard.

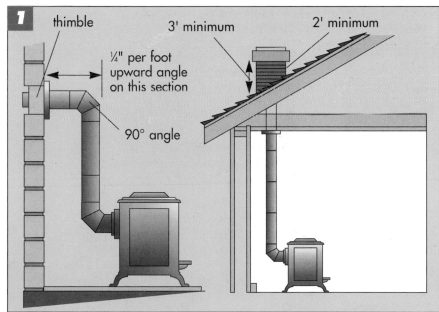

1. Plan the location.
Shown above are two options for venting a wood-burning stove. You can install a masonry flue in the wall, or extend a class-A metal flue up through the roof. Before you begin the project, check local requirements for chimney height above the roof line. Assemble the chimney and flue first, so you know exactly where the stove needs to be located. As you assemble the metal chimney, fit the sections together with the crimped ends pointing toward the stove. That way, any condensation will flow back to the fire and dissipate.

2. Lay out the job.

Following the manufacturer's recommendations and local codes, decide on the dimensions of your hearth and fire wall. Some stoves require that large floor and wall spaces be fire protected, while others have minimal requirements. You may want to cover large areas with tile because it looks attractive and is easy to clean. The dimensions shown at right are typical for a medium-sized woodstove.

Try to plan the layout so that you can use full tiles for the entire installation. Take into account the width of the grout joints.

Cut away any carpeting and padding. Remove a section of baseboard molding wide enough to accommodate the fire wall. If required by code, first attach ¼-inch-thick backerboard to the floor and wall. Screws on the wall should attach to studs.

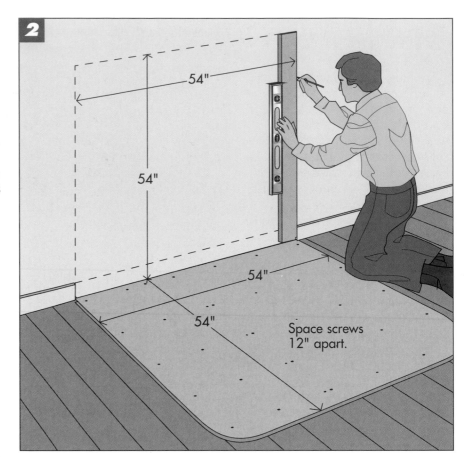

3. Set the tile.

Dry-fit the tiles for the hearth and for the first row on the wall. Move the hearth tiles out of the way. Mix thin-set mortar with liquid latex. When applying the tile to the wall, check for level and plumb with a carpenter's level. Use plastic spacers to maintain consistent joints between the tiles.

To set the hearth tiles, start in a corner and lay the row that meets the wall first, taking care to line up the hearth grout joints with the wall grout joints. If necessary, use a snap cutter to cut tiles. Wait a day for the tiles to set, then grout the joints.

TAKING TILE OUTDOORS

Tile can be a wonderful material for exterior patios, porches, pool surrounds, and walkways. In mild climates, tile has been used for thousands of years. In cold climates, however, tile has been used sparingly—and often unsuccessfully—outdoors. That is largely because the freeze-thaw cycle causes the ground to expand and contract beyond what a tile installation can endure.

Today, that concern is largely a thing of the past. New materials and installation techniques now allow tile to be used in cold climates with much greater success. Select tiles for patios, porches, and walkways that have a nonslip surface. Vitreous and impervious tiles absorb the least amount of water, making them better able to withstand freezing weather. In regions with a varied climate, all of the setting materials must be labeled as *freeze/thaw stable* for installations in cold climates.

ABOVE RIGHT: Unglazed pavers cut the glare in sunny locations and are an easy-to-maintain choice for outdoor living spaces in warm climates. Because of they absorb water, unglazed tiles can't withstand the freeze/thaw cycle of colder climates.

RIGHT: In addition to giving you a chance to add color and style to a pool, tile is less abrasive than concrete or brick, and so makes an ideal edging material for pools. Using it as a decorative feature in combination with brick and concrete keeps costs down. Installing tile in outdoor food preparation areas and on patios are good projects for do-it-yourselfers, but tiling a pool is a job for professionals.

LAYING A CONCRETE PATIO SUBSTRATE

Patios made of bricks or concrete pavers can be installed dry, on a bed of well-tamped sand. In warm climates, set thick tiles the same way. But in most locations, an outdoor tile surface needs to rest on a solid substrate of concrete.

Installing a new concrete slab is a major undertaking. Talk with a local building inspector and find out the requirements for your area; these regulations ensure that a slab will survive in your climate. In areas with severe winters, it is important to lay a well-tamped bed of gravel before pouring the concrete, so that water can drain away before it has a chance to puddle and freeze, cracking the concrete surface.

Here we show you how to install a surface that is smooth enough to receive tile. If the prospect of building forms and pouring concrete is daunting, hire a contractor to handle that part of the job for you. Do not tile over an existing concrete patio without first examining it, then preparing it (see page 99).

(see page 99)

YOU'LL NEED

TIME: With two helpers, one day to excavate, half a day to build forms, and a day to pour and finish the concrete.
SKILLS: Measuring and cutting wood, checking for square, driving stakes, fastening with nails or screws, screeding, finishing concrete (a special skill—have an experienced finisher at least give you advice).
TOOLS: Hammer, circular saw, carpenter's level, shovels, wheelbarrows, rake, straightedge, bull float or darby, broom, concrete finishing trowels.

1. Excavate the site.
Use mason's line and stakes to mark the perimeter and height of the new slab. Allow for the slab to slope down away from the house ¼ inch for every running foot. Remove the sod and topsoil to the desired depth. If you want to use the sod elsewhere, undercut it horizontally about 2 inches beneath the surface and cut it into easy-to-handle sections. Save enough to resod around the edges of the new slab. If you're putting gravel or sand under the slab, excavate at least 5 inches deep. Check the depth from time to time as you dig by laying a straight 2×4 or 2×6 on edge so its top barely touches the mason's line.

Stake forms every 3'-4'.

2. Install the forms.
Use straight 2×4s or 2×6s for the forms (depending on the desired slab thickness). Anchor the forms by driving 2×4 stakes, and pounding two double-headed nails through the stakes and into the form. Place your foot against the opposite side of the forms to make nailing easier. Be sure the tops of the forms are level with or above the tops of the stakes. Support each board with foot-long stakes every 3 to 4 feet. Make sure that the forms are square and properly sloped away from the house.

Divide a large slab.

Roll reinforcing mesh out, and cut it to fit. Adding dividers on a large patio allows you to pour and finish manageable amounts of concrete. If the dividers will be temporary, use any straight length of lumber. If you plan to leave the divider in as part of the slab, use pressure-treated lumber or redwood. At right, two 2×2s sandwich the mesh, keeping it at the right height for maximum effectiveness.

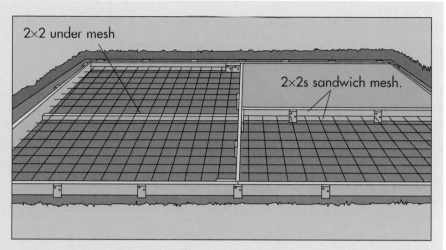

2×2 under mesh

2×2s sandwich mesh.

Protect permanent dividers.

Install permanent dividers every 12 feet. Brush on a coat of wood sealer to enhance rot resistance. Put masking tape on the top edges to keep wet concrete from staining the wood and to avoid scratching the forms when you screed. Drive interior stakes 1 inch below the top of the permanent dividers so they will not be visible once the concrete is poured.

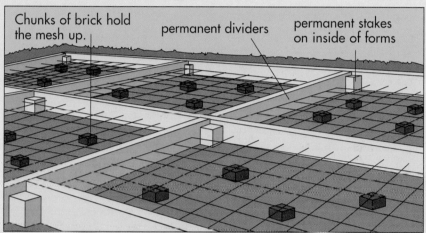

Chunks of brick hold the mesh up.

permanent dividers

permanent stakes on inside of forms

Position the ramp to clear the form.

3. Transport the concrete on ramps.
Mix your concrete as near to the site as possible; do not use curing compounds. Or have the ready-mix truck park as close as is safe. (A concrete truck weighs enough to crack sidewalks and driveways.) Wet concrete is heavy: Keep wheelbarrow loads small enough to handle. To cross soft soil or lawns, lay a walkway of 2×10 or 2×12 planks. Build ramps over the forms so you do not disturb them. Use two or more wheelbarrows to keep the job moving.

4. Dump and move the concrete.
Start dumping concrete in the farthest corner of the forms. Dump it in mounds that reach ½ inch or so above the top of the form. It helps to have one person working a shovel while others run the wheelbarrows. The shoveler directs the wheelbarrow handlers and tells them where to dump the concrete. Wear gloves and heavy boots that fit snugly. Pace your efforts because you'll be moving a lot of concrete before the pour is complete.

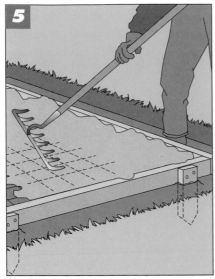

5. Pull up reinforcing mesh.

While pouring the concrete, use a hoe, rake, or shovel to pull the wire mesh up into the concrete. For the greatest strength, keep the mesh positioned halfway between the bottom of the excavation and the finished surface of the slab. Watch that the mesh doesn't get pushed against the form at any point. Keep it 1 to 2 inches away from all forms.

6. Tamp concrete to remove air pockets.

For best results, the concrete should adhere to the forms and dividers and contain no air pockets. Run a shovel up and down along the inside edge of all forms and tap the sides of the forms with a hammer. Be sure to check that all corners are filled in and tamped adequately.

7. Screed with a straightedge.

Begin screeding (leveling) as soon as you've filled the first 3 or 4 feet of the length of the form. Keep both ends of the screed—a straight 2×4—pressed down on the top of the form while moving it back and forth in a sawing motion and drawing it toward the unleveled concrete. If depressions occur, fill in with concrete and screed again.

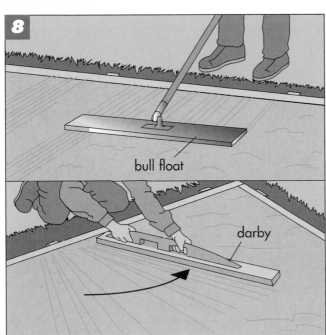

8. Float the surface.

Screed a second time to make sure the surface is level. To smooth the surface, run a bull float in long, back-and-forth motions, slightly raising its leading edge so it does not dig into the concrete. If you use a darby, work in large, sweeping arcs.

9. Broom the finish.

For a smooth finish, professionals use a steel trowel. For a tiling finish, a broom finish is fine. Dampen the broom, and pull it only—do not push it. Have a brick or piece of 2×4 handy so you can tap the broom now and then to keep it clean.

PREPARING A CONCRETE SURFACE

You can tile over an existing concrete patio that's in good condition as long as it is at least 3 inches thick, sloped to allow water to drain off, and free of serious cracks. If the patio has a crack that keeps growing every year, or if one side of the crack is higher than the other, then it has structural problems. Don't tile over a slab in such a condition. Also, see that the slab is sitting slightly above ground level and is cleaned of any oil, dirt, and curing compounds.

YOU'LL NEED

TIME: An hour for most patches.
SKILLS: Spreading patching compound smoothly.
TOOLS: Concrete trowel, mason's trowel, 2×4, grinding tool, hose, stiff brush.

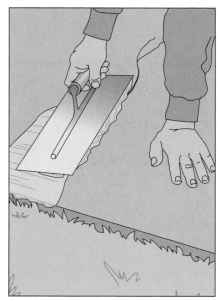

Patch cracks.
Fill small cracks or other irregularities with a concrete patching compound. Latex and epoxy compounds work well. Or use sand-mix concrete mixed with latex additive.

Fill in low spots.
Use a straightedge to locate low spots on a patio. Screed a patching or self-leveling compound over the low spots to create a flat surface. Finish with a trowel and/or broom to match the surrounding surface.

Repair edges.
If concrete is broken along the edges of the patio, chip away any loose concrete, clean, and wet the area. Place a board along the damaged area, then fill with patching compound or fresh mortar. Smooth with a trowel and allow to set.

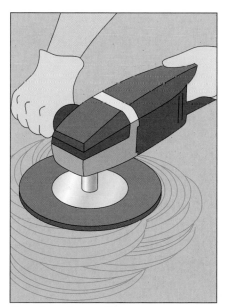

Roughen the surface.
If the patio has a smooth, steel-troweled finish, you will have to roughen the surface before tiling. Use a grinding tool with an abrasive wheel; or a tool-rental store may have a special tool for the job.

Clean the surface.
Scrub the surface with water and a stiff brush. Use a degreaser to remove oil and grease stains. If the patio is smooth and dirty, rent a power washer with at least 4,000 psi to clean and roughen the surface simultaneously.

LAYING PATIO TILE

An outdoor tile surface comes under a good deal of stress, so use the best-quality materials available for each step. Talk with your tile dealer about specific products that will perform best outdoors. Don't give water any chance to enter or hide beneath your tiled surface. Pack the grout joints as tightly as possible, then seal them carefully. Renew the grout sealer and caulk or sealant in expansion joints regularly.

YOU'LL NEED

TIME: About a day to install 100 square feet of tile; a few hours 1 to 2 days later to grout it.
SKILLS: Cutting and installing tile.
TOOLS: Notched trowel, snap cutter or wet saw, rubber mallet, grouting float, sponge.

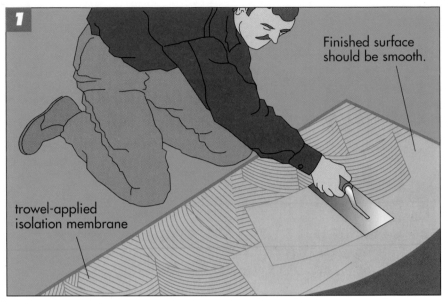

Finished surface should be smooth.

trowel-applied isolation membrane

1. Apply an isolation membrane.
A trowel-applied isolation membrane is a caulklike substance that never fully hardens. It forms a layer that separates the tile from the patio, making it less likely that cracks in the concrete will translate to the grout and tile. Apply it with the notched side of the trowel to ensure an even and level coating, then smooth it with the flat side.

2. Dry-set the tiles.
Allow the isolation membrane to cure. Lay the tiles (pages 31–33) in a dry run over at least part of the surface before mixing any adhesive; this is particularly important if you will be setting tiles in a pattern. If the patio is slightly out of square, dry-setting gives you a chance to judge how best to arrange and cut tiles.

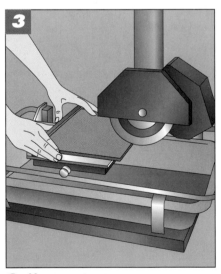

3. Use a wet saw.
For thick tile or stone, or to cut inside corners accurately, rent a wet saw. It quickly and cleanly slices through the hardest of materials, even granite. To keep the blade from getting dull, keep water running on it at all times.

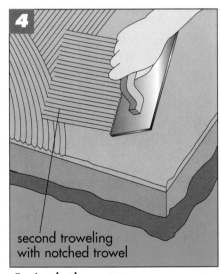

second troweling with notched trowel

4. Apply the mortar.
Use thin-set mortar mixed with a liquid latex additive. Apply the mortar in two steps. Trowel on a smooth base coat about ½ inch thick. Then comb the surface with the notched side of the trowel, taking care that the notches do not penetrate through to the concrete base. Use long, sweeping strokes.

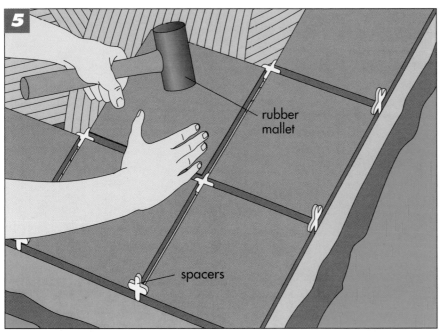

rubber
mallet

spacers

5. Set the tile.

Give each tile a twist as you push it into the adhesive. Take care not to slide the tile into position. Use spacers to keep the tiles aligned. If the tiles are not flush, use a beating block and hammer or a rubber mallet to gently tap them into alignment.

EXPERTS' INSIGHT

EXPANSION JOINTS

Tile is going to expand and contract on a patio installation even more than it will indoors. You can minimize damage due to this movement by placing expansion joints between tiles no more than 16 feet apart and wherever the tile meets another surface, such as the foundation of the house or stairs. Ideally, an expansion joint should fall over a similar joint in the concrete pad. After grouting the other joints, fill the expansion joints with caulk or sealant.

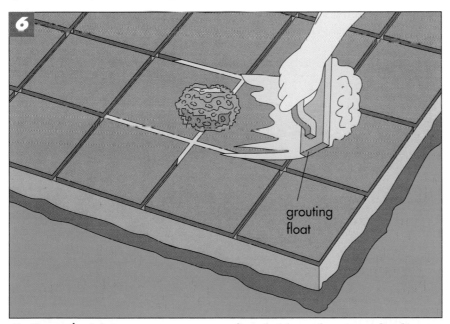

grouting
float

6. Grout the joints.

Allow time for the adhesive to set (usually one or two days). Mix the grout of your choice, using latex additive to keep it from cracking later on. Push the grout into the joints with a grouting float, making sure you move the float in at least two directions at all points. Once the joints in a small section are fully packed, scrape with the float held nearly perpendicular to the tiles to remove as much excess as possible. Clean the grout from the tile surface and make smooth grout lines, first by laying a wet towel on the surface and pulling it toward you, then by wiping carefully with a damp sponge. Sponge-clean the surface several times. After the surface has dried, buff with a dry towel.

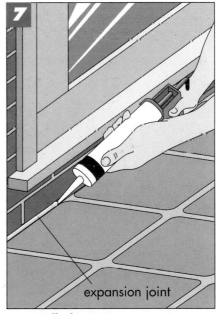

expansion joint

7. Caulk the expansion joints.

Choose a caulk or sealant that closely matches the grout in color. Clean the joints of any adhesive that may have squeezed up, then clean and vacuum the joint. Neatly run a bead of caulk or sealant along the expansion joints. Shape the joints, if you like, with the back side of a spoon, a dampened rag, or your finger.

TILING OUTDOOR STEPS

Although not often used in new construction today, tiled stairs used to be a popular choice in homebuilding. You can add tile to both the risers and the treads of a concrete stairway. On a wood stairway, a popular choice is to install tiles on the risers only. Risers are not stepped on, so they can be covered with thin wall tiles if you prefer. Cover the entire riser, or use a few decorative tiles to accent. Large, unglazed paver or quarry tiles are attractive for exterior treads. The tiles should be at least ½ inch thick and slip resistant. Special bullnose tiles are available that can extend over the riser. Install riser tiles before you install the tread tiles.

YOU'LL NEED

TIME: About one day to install tiles on a typical front entry, plus an hour or two to grout.
SKILLS: Installing floor tile, cutting, and installing plywood or backerboard.
TOOLS: Tape measure, saw, hammer, drill, tiling and grouting tools.

CAUTION!
SAFE STAIR DIMENSIONS
Before tiling over stairs, make sure they are safe. The treads, the surface you step on, should be about 11 inches deep; although for exterior stairs it is often recommended that they be deeper. The riser, the vertical element between treads, should be about 7 inches high. Check with your building department if you are not sure about your stair dimensions.

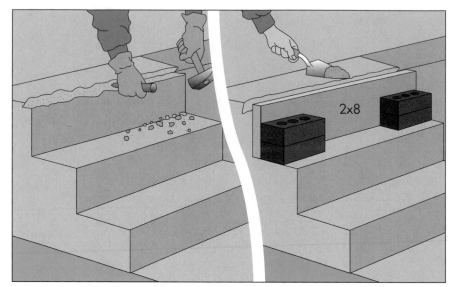

Prepare concrete stairs.
Concrete stairs are the best surface for tile. But the concrete must be in solid condition, with no major cracks or other structural damage. Seal small cracks with a concrete patching compound. Repair damaged edges by chipping away any loose concrete, then sweeping and wetting the area. Place a board along the damaged area, then fill it with patching compound or fresh mortar. Smooth with a trowel and allow to set.

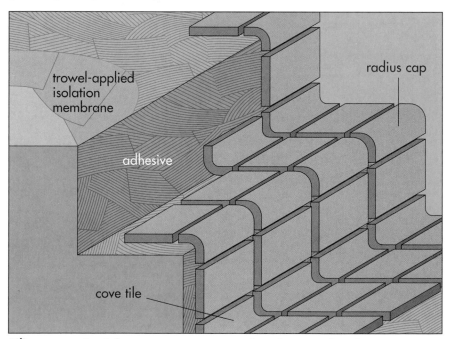

Tiling concrete stairs.
The most professional installation calls for a new mortar setting bed applied over the entire surface. But you can also tile over concrete stairs following the general guidelines for a concrete patio (see pages 96–98). Remove oily stains and make sure that the concrete does not contain curing compounds. Spread a trowel-applied isolation membrane before setting tiles. Use radius cap and cove tiles as shown to strengthen the edges and make cleanup easier.

EXPERTS' INSIGHT

SLIP RESISTANCE

The best choice for the treads on stairs is slip-resistant tile; at the very least, use unglazed tile. See if your tile dealer carries tiles made for use on stairs. For extra safety, buy special slip-resistant inserts for the tread edges. These typically consist of a metal channel, part of which slips under the tread, with a replaceable plastic or rubber insert that covers the nosing. To reduce slippage on a step surface that is already installed, add glue-on strips.

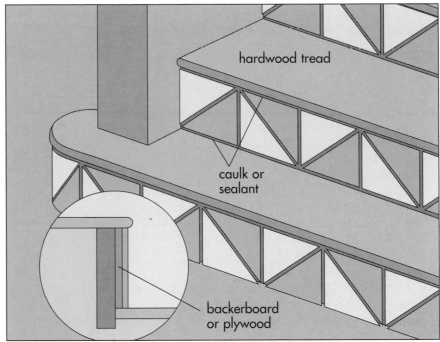

Tile the risers only.
Combine tiled risers with hardwood treads for an appealing contrast. Use standard wall tiles or natural stone tiles. If possible, install plywood or backerboard for a smooth substrate. Set the tiles in adhesive, and seal the top and bottom edges with caulk or sealant rather than grout.

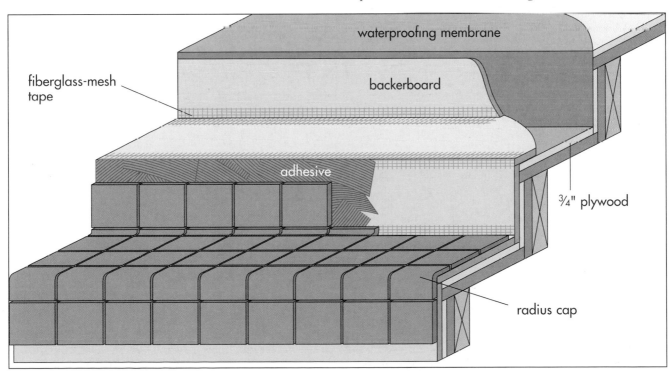

Tiling over wood stairs.
Take special care here to ensure that the substrate will not flex when walked on. The stair frame must be solid, inflexible, and in good condition. Cover the treads, risers, and any landings with exterior-grade ³⁄₄-inch plywood. Then lay waterproofing membrane over the whole job. Install backerboard over the membrane. Use only tiles and setting materials suitable for exterior installations. Use bullnose caps wherever a tile edge is exposed. If you are planning to tile over an existing stair, you may have to adjust the heights of the landings at the top and bottom to keep the stairs safe and up to code.

CLEANING TILE

Aside from its beauty and durability, one of the big advantages of tile is that it is so easy to clean. If you attend to routine cleaning—immediately wiping up spills that could stain, cleaning and sealing grout—you may never have to use any but the most common household products to keep your tile looking as good as new for years. Sweep or vacuum tile floors regularly. Use rugs or floor mats at entryways and other heavily traveled areas. On tiled countertops, use placemats and coasters under plates and glasses. If you must scrub a surface, avoid using metal scouring pads—woven-plastic scrubbers are much safer. And never mix different types of cleaning solutions (for example, chlorine bleach and ammonia).

Routine cleaning and maintenance. Wipe up spills immediately. Prepare a solution of warm water and dishwashing detergent or white vinegar, and thoroughly clean the tiled surface with a mop or sponge. For stubborn dirt, use an all-purpose household (soap-free) cleaner or a commercial tile cleaner. Rinse with clean water.

Keep grout clean. Grout is the most demanding element of your tile floor. Coat the grout with a good-quality grout sealer after the grout has cured on a new installation. Reapply the sealer about every six months, or when the grout becomes porous and hard to clean.

Cleaning stone tiles. Sweep or vacuum regularly. Wipe with a damp mop, warm water, and a little dishwashing detergent. Rinse thoroughly with clean water. Do not use abrasive, scented, or solvent-based cleaners.

Cleaning tubs and showers. If routine cleaning doesn't remove soap and lime buildup, use a commercial bathroom cleaner or all-purpose cleaner. To remove caked-on dirt, leave the cleaner on the surface for a while before wiping it off. Prevent mildew by scrubbing grout joints with a solution of water and bleach.

REMOVING STAINS

Glazed tile is very resistant to staining; if it becomes discolored, then the glazing has failed. Unglazed tiles such as quarry tile and stone, however, can become badly stained. Prevention is the best remedy: Follow the cleaning tips on page 104, and perhaps even apply a coat of acrylic finish to a very porous tile surface that is most likely to become stained.

Often the best way to clean stains on tile is to make a paste, for example, of scouring powder and water. A thick paste will scour better than regular cleaner, and if you let it sit on the stain for several hours, it will continue to soak up unwanted color. On greasy stains, a paste made of cat-box litter and water can also work.

Though tile is strong and hard, take care not to scratch its surface. Use nylon scrubbers rather than steel wool, and take care when scraping with a metal tool.

REMOVING STAINS

Coffee, tea, blood, mustard, wine, fruit juice, rust, lipstick
Mix baking soda with a little water to create a thick paste. Rub the paste on the stain, and leave it until dry. Rinse and wipe dry. For deep, stubborn stains, apply full-strength household chlorine bleach. As a last resort, use an acid-based cleaner as directed on the label.

Oil, grease, tar
To remove oily stains from pavers, brick, or tiles made from concrete, prepare a liquid mixture of plaster of paris. Brush the mixture on the stain and let it rest for 24 hours. Brush off and rinse. Repeat if necessary. Alternately, use a commercial concrete or driveway cleaner.

Paint
Wipe a commercial paint remover on the paint, then carefully scrape off the paint with a razor knife.

Mineral deposits
Wipe with white vinegar or mix a solution of half water and half ammonia. Rinse and pat dry.

Cooking fats and grease
Clean with a concentrated solution of all-purpose household cleaner.

CAUTION!
PROTECT YOURSELF AGAINST CHEMICALS
If you must resort to a toxic or highly caustic product to remove a particularly stubborn stain, exercise extreme caution. Read and follow the instructions on the label. Wear rubber gloves and eye protection, and provide sufficient ventilation so that you don't have to inhale the fumes. Wear old clothes—they might get bleach stains or even develop holes. Use these products when children are out of the house, or at least when they can be kept a safe distance away.

Remove mildew.
Use a toothbrush dipped in household chlorine bleach to remove mildew stains. To remove the chlorine odor, wipe with a solution of baking soda and water.

Reserve acid cleaners.
Use acid cleaners only as a last resort to remove stains or grout haze that was allowed to dry on the tile. Muriatic acid is the most common. Start with a weak solution, and increase the strength if that doesn't work. Protect your eyes and skin, and wear a charcoal-filter mask.

REPLACING GROUT

*B*efore you start repairing grout joints, try to determine the source of the problem. Loose or cracked grout over a fairly large area may indicate a structural problem below the surface, whereas a few gaps or cracks may be due to a sloppy grouting job in that area. If the grout has been in bad shape for some time, you should try to determine if water has managed to pass through the substrate, which can cause tiles to buckle and may even lead to structural problems.

YOU'LL NEED

TIME: A couple of hours for spot repairs, 1–2 days for a large regrouting job.
SKILLS: Careful sawing or digging out of old grout, grouting.
TOOLS: Grout saw, grouting float, sponge, bucket, dry cloth.

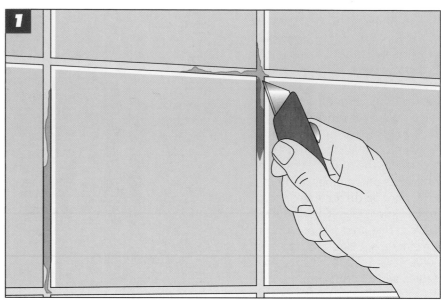

1. Remove old grout.
Remove grout with a utility knife or an old hacksaw blade. For very narrow joints, use the tip of an awl. If you have to remove a lot of grout, the job will go much faster with a grout saw (available at tile dealers and large home centers), small handheld tile saw, or angle grinder equipped with a diamond blade (see page 47). Vacuum the joints and clean the tiles to remove dirt, oil, or soap scum.

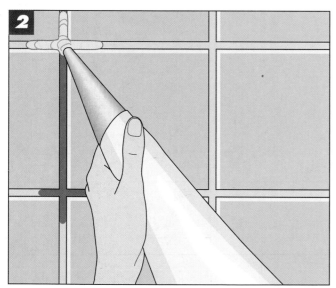

2. Apply new grout.
Unless you are regrouting the entire installation, try to match the color of the new grout with the old. (Take a loose piece of grout with you when you go shopping.) If you have doubts about the color, mix a small amount and let it dry. After 2 or 3 days, compare the colors. Mix the grout with a latex additive before applying. The additive will waterproof and help prevent cracks in the future. Apply small amounts of grout with a grout bag or your finger.

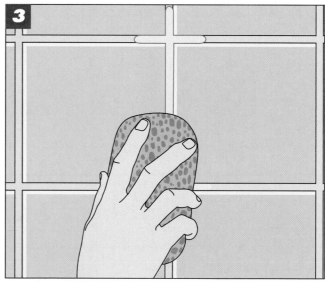

3. Clean and seal.
Clean the grout using a dampened sponge to wipe the tiles. Wipe with a circular motion, making sure the grout joints are consistent in depth. Rinse your sponge often. Let the grout dry for several days before applying a grout sealer.

REPLACING TILE

*I*f a number of tiles have come loose, your main job may be to repair a substrate that has been water damaged. Remove as many tiles as necessary so you can firm up any soft parts of the substrate; patch with backerboard. If you are working near a tub or sink, be sure to cover the tub and especially the drain, to prevent scratches and a clogged drain.

It may be difficult to find a replacement tile. If you don't have any spare tiles left from the original installation, take a piece with you to the store and find tiles that match in size and color.

YOU'LL NEED

TIME: 1–2 hours to replace a tile.
SKILLS: Handling a chisel and hammer, setting tile.
TOOLS: Hammer, cold chisel, putty knife.

1. Remove old tile.
If the tile doesn't simply pop out, put on safety glasses and break the connection with adjacent tiles by sawing through the grout joint around the tile (see page 106). With your hammer, tap at the damaged tile to crack it into smaller pieces. Don't hit too hard, or you could damage the substrate or shake other tiles loose. Use a cold chisel with the hammer to chip away the tiles. Work the chisel from the center out, taking care to avoid damaging other tiles.

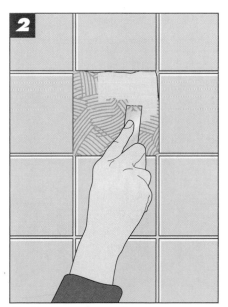

2. Prepare the surface.
Use a putty knife or margin trowel to scrape away all of the old adhesive. Remove any remaining grout from the joints. Create a smooth, clean surface for the new tile.

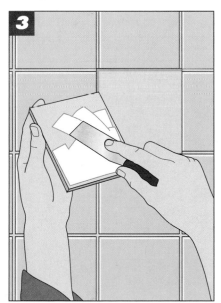

3. Install new tile.
Use the same adhesive as was used on the original installation. If you don't know what it was, use an adhesive appropriate to the installation (see page 23). Spread a thin coat of the adhesive over the entire back of the replacement tile. Spread another coat on the setting

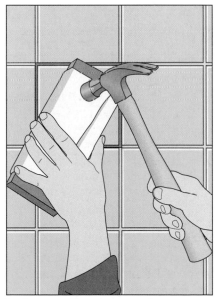

bed. Press the tile into place, giving it a gentle twist. Use a beating block and hammer to set the tile flush. If necessary, hold the tile in place with masking tape. Wait 1 or 2 days before grouting, then wait several more days and seal the grout (see pages 48-51).

GLOSSARY

For words not listed here, or for more about those that are, refer to the index, pages 110–112.

Actual dimension. The true size of a tile. See *nominal dimension.*

Backsplash. Typically, a 3- to 4-inch-high length of material at the back edge of a countertop extending the full length.

Backerboard. A ready-made surface for setting tile. Also called cement board. Can be cement-based or gypsum-based.

Beating block. Used to press tiles evenly into adhesive. Can be a store-bought rubber-faced model or a piece of plywood that you've covered with terry cloth.

Building codes. Community ordinances governing the manner in which a home or other structure may be constructed or modified. Most codes deal primarily with fire and health concerns and have separate sections relating to electrical, plumbing, and structural work.

Bullnose tiles. Can also be called caps. Tiles shaped to define the edges of an installation.

Buttering or back buttering. Applying mortar on bricks or blocks with a trowel before laying.

Butt joint. The joint formed by two pieces of material when fastened end to end, end to face, or end to edge.

Casing. The trimming around a door, window, or other opening.

Caulk. Any one of a variety of compounds used to seal seams and joints against infiltration of water and air.

Cement board. A backerboard with a mesh coat, cement board is a surface for setting tile.

Ceramic tile. Made from refined clay usually mixed with additives and water and hardened in a kiln. Can be glazed or unglazed.

Darby. A long-bladed wood float commonly used to smooth the surface of freshly poured concrete in situations where using a smaller float isn't practical.

Drywall. A basic interior building material consisting of big sheets of pressed gypsum faced with heavy paper on both sides. Also known as gypsum board, plasterboard, and Sheetrock (a trade name). Moisture-resistant drywall is known as green or blue board.

Expansion joint. The space built into a structure between two surfaces or structural elements to allow materials to expand and contract during temperature changes without damage.

Field tiles. Flat tiles, in contrast to trim tiles that are shaped to turn corners or define the edges of an installation.

Float. A rectangular wood or metal hand tool that is used for smoothing and compressing wet concrete.

Flush. On the same plane as, or level with, a surrounding surface.

Glazing. A protective and decorative coating, often colored, that is fired onto the surface of some tiles.

Granite. A quartz-based stone with a tough, glossy appearance; granite is harder than marble.

Greenboard. Similar to regular drywall, this material is moisture resistant, though not waterproof. Also referred to as *blueboard.*

Grout. A thin mortar mixture used to fill the joints between tiles. Also, to apply grout. (See also *mortar.*)

Grouting float. A rubber-backed trowel used for pressing the grout into the joints.

Impervious tile. Tiles least likely to absorb water which are generally used in hospitals, restaurants, and other commercial locations.

Inside corner. The point at which two walls form an internal angle, as in the corner of a room.

Isolation membrane. A sub-surface layer for tile installations. Chlorinated polyethylene (CPE) sheets are used for an isolation membrane.

Jamb. The top and side frames of a door or window opening.

Joint compound. A synthetic formula used in combination with paper tape to conceal joints between drywall panels.

Level. When any surface is at true horizontal. Also a tool used to determine level.

Marble. A hard and durable limestone characterized by varied patterns and colors of veins.

Masonry cement. A special mix of portland cement and hydrated lime used for preparing mortar. The lime adds to the workability of the mortar.

Membrane. A sub-surface layer for tile installations. Tar paper is used for a waterproofing membrane. Chlorinated polyethylene (CPE) sheets are used for an isolation membrane.

Mexican paver. Unglazed tile most often used on floors.

Mortar. A mixture of masonry cement, masonry sand, and water. For most jobs, the proportion of cement to sand is 1:3. Also, to apply mortar.

Mosaic tile. Small (1 or 2 inch) vitreous squares or hexagons, mounted on sheets or joined with adhesive strips.

Nominal dimension. The stated size of a tile, which usually includes a standard grout joint. The actual dimension is somewhat smaller.

Nonvitreous tile. Porous ceramic tiles that should be used indoors in dry locations.

Organic mastic. A premixed setting adhesive for tiles. Used often on walls because it holds tiles in place without slippage.

Outside corners. The point at which two walls form an external angle, the corner you can usually walk around.

Particleboard. Panels made from compressed wood chips and glue.

Pavers. Vitreous floor tiles, usually $3/8$ inch thick and glazed or unglazed.

Plumb. When a surface is at true vertical.

Plumb bob. Weight used with a plumb line to align vertical points and determine plumb.

Quarry tile. Unglazed, vitreous tiles, usually $1/2$-inch thick, used on floors.

Rod saw. A strip of tungsten carbide that fits into a standard hacksaw body. It is used for cutting tight curves in tile.

Screed. To use a straightedge, often a 2×4 or 2×6, for leveling concrete as it is poured into a form.

Sealant. Coating used to protect tile and grout from water infiltration.

Semivitreous tile. Semiporous ceramic tiles that can be used indoors, in dry to occasionally wet locations.

Shower pan. The floor of a shower stall which houses the drain. Can be a prefabricated unit made of fiberglass, acrylic, terrazzo, or other materials.

Slate. A rough-surfaced tile that has been split, rather than sliced, from quarried stone.

Snap cutter. Cutting tool for tile. Resembles a glass cutter, except that it is mounted on a guide bar.

Spacers. Small pieces of plastic that are used to ensure consistent grout-joint width between tiles.

Square. The condition that exists when one surface is at a 90-degree angle to another. Also a tool used to determine square.

Straightedge. An improvised tool, usually a 1×4 or 2×4 with a straight edge, used to mark a straight line on material or to determine if a surface is even.

Stone tile. Marble, granite, flagstone, and slate. Dimensioned (or gauged) stone is cut to uniform size. Hand-split (or cleft) stone varies in size.

Subfloor. Usually plywood or another sheet material covering the floor joists.

Substrate. The setting bed and any other layers beneath a tile surface.

Taping. The process of covering drywall joints with tape and joint compound.

Terrazzo tiles. Small pieces of granite or marble set in mortar, then polished.

Thin-set mortar. A setting adhesive for tiles.

Tile nippers. Cutting tool for making small notches and curves in tile. Resemble pliers, but have carbide-tipped edges.

Toenail. To drive a nail at an angle to hold together two pieces of material.

Trim tile. Tiles that are shaped to turn corners or define the edges of an installation. Includes cove trim, bullnose, V-cap, quarter round, inside corner, and outside corner.

Trowel. Any of several flat and oblong or pointed metal tools used for handling adhesive and grout and/or concrete and mortar.

Vitreous tile. Ceramic tiles with a low porosity, used indoors or outdoors, in wet or dry locations.

Wet saw. A power tool for cutting tile. A pump sprays water to cool the diamond-tipped blade and remove chips.

INDEX

METRIC CONVERSIONS

U.S. UNITS TO METRIC EQUIVALENTS			METRIC UNITS TO U.S. EQUIVALENTS		
To Convert From	Multiply By	To Get	To Convert From	Multiply By	To Get
Inches	25.4	Millimeters	Millimeters	0.0394	Inches
Inches	2.54	Centimeters	Centimeters	0.3937	Inches
Feet	30.48	Centimeters	Centimeters	0.0328	Feet
Feet	0.3048	Meters	Meters	3.2808	Feet
Yards	0.9144	Meters	Meters	1.0936	Yards
Miles	1.6093	Kilometers	Kilometers	0.6214	Miles
Square inches	6.4516	Square centimeters	Square centimeters	0.1550	Square inches
Square feet	0.0929	Square meters	Square meters	10.764	Square feet
Square yards	0.8361	Square meters	Square meters	1.1960	Square yards
Acres	0.4047	Hectares	Hectares	2.4711	Acres
Square miles	2.5899	Square kilometers	Square kilometers	0.3861	Square miles
Cubic inches	16.387	Cubic centimeters	Cubic centimeters	0.0610	Cubic inches
Cubic feet	0.0283	Cubic meters	Cubic meters	35.315	Cubic feet
Cubic feet	28.316	Liters	Liters	0.0353	Cubic feet
Cubic yards	0.7646	Cubic meters	Cubic meters	1.308U	Cubic yards
Cubic yards	764.55	Liters	Liters	0.0013	Cubic yards
Fluid ounces	29.574	Milliliters	Milliliters	0.0338	Fluid ounces
Quarts	0.9464	Liters	Liters	1.0567	Quarts
Gallons	3.7854	Liters	Liters	0.2642	Gallons
Drams	1.7718	Grams	Grams	0.5644	Drams
Ounces	28.350	Grams	Grams	0.0353	Ounces
Pounds	0.4536	Kilograms	Kilograms	2.2046	Pounds

To convert from degrees Fahrenheit (F) to degrees Celsius (C), first subtract 32, then multiply by ⁵⁄₉.

To convert from degrees Celsius to degrees Fahrenheit, multiply by ⁹⁄₅, then add 32.